A.S. JUDKINS, PH.D.

MICHAEL MCDANIEL, TH.D.

# ALIEN AGENDA

## THE RETURN
## OF THE
## NEPHILIM

# ALIEN AGENDA:
# THE RETURN OF THE NEPHILIM

ISBN 978-1-105-68625-2

1. UFOs     2. Eschatology     3. Philosophy

Book Cover Art & Design by John Shallenberger.

Edited by Tommy Bass, Milton Billiet, & Dick Wilson.

Pictures by A.S. Judkins, istockphoto.com & shutterstock.com.

Graphics by Henry Johnson. Engravings by Gustave Doré.


PUBLISHED BY

MAVERICK PUBLISHING CO.

GLEN ROSE, TEXAS

PRINTED IN THE USA

FIRST EDITION

This work is dedicated to our friend and colleague -

the late Dr. Clifford Wilson (1923-2012).


Well Done!

# Acknowledgments

**A.S. Judkins**- I would like to thank the late Dr. Clifford Wilson for his life service to the ministry and for believing in me. To Dr. McDaniel, co-author of this book, for his diligent study and teaching the word of God that has rooted me in the faith. To Dr. Carl Baugh, for making such an impact in my life to inspire me to go beyond what I thought I could not accomplish. To my family and friends who have supported me diligently through this effort. And to my Lord and Savior who is the author and finisher of my faith.

**Michael McDaniel**- I once heard Jack Hyles say, "You are who you have been becoming." Who I have become and what I understand about the Bible has been a process that includes many people. But I will only mention two; my father and mother. Because of their influence, I trusted Jesus Christ as my all-sufficient Savior at the age of 8. Again, their influence held sway when I decided in college to change my major from pre-law to ministry- a decision I have never regretted. I am so grateful to my heavenly Father for my parents who had a heart for God. Thank God, by His matchless grace, this "twice-dead" Gentile has been given the honor and privilege of laboring with Him both in His business now on this earth and in eternity in the heavenly places.

# Foreword

As a combat pilot with thousands of flying hours the closest encounter I've ever experienced with a UFO was being jumped by a Russian MIG 21 in Vietnam. Imagine my relief when I realized I was under attack by the North Vietnamese Air Force and not another worldly presence. The UFO phenomena is as real as that MIG but with one exception. It is more frightening. It is more frightening because the truth about UFOs may reveal things about our existence many will refuse to accept. Denial is such a powerful phenomenon.

One of the largest UFO "Flaps" ever recorded began in January 2008 in and around the north Texas town of Stephenville. Stephenville is located about 75 miles southwest of Fort Worth and about 15 miles from my home. During the "Flap" I never saw anything resembling a UFO. However, I did talk to many people who claim they saw "UFO's" and they were as serious as a heart attack. They believed it with every fiber of their body. I also believe they saw something. And it was something *they had never seen before!* Some testified they watched the crafts for many minutes at close range. Many took pictures. Without exception they believed they saw something from a planet somewhere in the universe and it wasn't Earth. They are not alone. UFOs have been reported since the beginning of recorded history and it has always been assumed they are from another world. Are they from outer space? If not from outer space then where do they come from? How long did it take them to get here? How long does it take them to get back? After they mutilate a few cows and put on an air show where do they go? Why were they here? Do they have a purpose? Does the Bible have any insight into their existence?

You are holding in your hand one of the most distinctive books about UFOs you will ever read. The authors are personal friends, who I know to be reasonable people who approach the UFO phenomena in a logical, analytical, and uniquely *Biblical* fashion. This book has the potential to completely change your attitude toward UFOs and the people who see them. You won't be able to put it down. I hope you will share it with your friends, your church, your golf club, and with anyone else who has an interest in the subject. Put your preconceived notions aside and enjoy this fascinating ride.

Colonel (RET) Rick Davis

# Preface

"There is a principle which is a bar against all information, which is proof against all argument, and which cannot fail to keep man in everlasting ignorance. That principle is condemnation before investigation." — Edmund Spencer

You may have noticed over the last 50 years that Hollywood movies have increasingly moved into New Age concepts. These concepts embrace aliens, life on other planets, and the UFO phenomena. Since the early days of Star Trek, Star Wars, Battle Star Galactica and Buck Rogers in the 21st Century, the film and TV industry has promoted the belief that we are not alone in the universe. Today, movies like Contact, Men in Black, War of the Worlds, Independence Day and Prometheus are mainstream. What was once unimaginable is now widely accepted as a viable reality. But why would people be so willing to accept alien life? Is there credible evidence suggesting that we are not alone? Are ETs out there? What are the implications if contact is made? More importantly however, people are really asking the four great questions of life.

Who am I?
Where did I come from?
What is my purpose here?
Where am I going?

As we go through 2012 and beyond, people are asking questions about life origins. Unfortunately, the majority of people cannot answer the four great questions of life. People are searching for the truth. As

Christians, we are to be both salt and light so that we may share the hope and purpose within us. We are to be instant in season and out of season, ready to give an answer to questions such as these. This is the very reason that we are putting forth this information; to answer these questions from a Biblical perspective. There are very few people addressing this issue from this angle. It is time that someone stands for the truth and unveils the deception. Yes, there is a deception and it will only get worse as we race towards the End Times. This book will give you a keen insight to the truth about the Alien Agenda and the return of the Nephilim.

# Table of Contents

## Chapter 1

# UFO's:

# Fact or Fiction?

As we look at the UFO phenomena, you should know right from the start that the issue at stake here is authority. For the Bible-believing Christian, there is one final authority by which we can judge everything in life. That authority is the Bible. You may think that this point is irrelevant to our discussion of UFOs. I assure you, it's not. It is at the very heart of the issue, which you shall soon see. We will examine UFOs, their proponents and opponents by the Word of God, just as we can use it to examine all matters of life. But this examination is not accepted by man. The secular world dislikes any person who uses the

Bible as a standard for judgment of the things and people in this world. There has been a concerted effort to overthrow the authority of God's Word for thousands of years and that effort will continue until the end of this Age.

There are 3 reasons for this attempt to overthrow the Bible:

1. The Bible puts the emphasis in history on the person and work of "one man;" not science and education (for every reference to any other person in the Bible, there are 35 references to Jesus- and they will not tolerate Jesus unless he is just one more in a line of many others).

2. Because the Bible takes a negative view of evolution (you have to get rid of the Bible in order to teach evolution as religious doctrine. The leaders of NEA, HEW, and the UN are all evolutionists. How will they bring peace on earth with the Bible standing in the way? They have to get rid of the Bible as the standard of judgment and substitute something like science, religion, experience, feelings or world courts. In order to accomplish this they must destroy people's faith in the Bible as a standard for judging things in this world.

3. Because of the Bible's negative view of man due to sin.

> **Psalms 51:5 (KJV)**
> 5 Behold, I was shapen in iniquity; and in sin did my mother conceive me.

> **Genesis 6:5 (KJV)**
> 5 And God saw that the wickedness of man was great in the earth and that every imagination of the thoughts of his heart was only evil continually.

The unsaved man is convinced that he is as good as anyone else if he just sets his mind to it. He thinks if he just does this and that he is as good as anyone who may not do the things he does and as good as those who do things that he cannot do. The point is this; God did intervene when he sent his Son into the world to release us from the power of sin because there was absolutely nothing we could do our own that would undo the fact that we are sinners by nature and our hearts are evil. So attempts are made to overthrow the Bible so people can convince themselves of the inherent goodness of man. As one famous atheist said, "this world isn't big enough for the Bible and atheism; one or the other has got to go!" Since we know the agenda that is at work here, we are going to use the Bible to examine the UFO phenomena and the information we have about them just as we use it to examine everything else in the world.

You should also know that the current secular teachings regarding UFOs undermine almost everything you have ever known about the Bible. In order for them to teach the current consensus regarding UFOs, they have to take Genesis 3 and reinterpret it to say that the serpent had Eve's best interest at heart and was trying to help mankind back in the Garden of Eden! How absurd!

UFOs also have a religious overtone to them. They are referenced to the Bible, Ezekiel, Jesus Christ and the book of Genesis by every writer of UFO material. Practically all of the books, magazines and materials regarding UFOs and their interaction with mankind, the majority are shown to be something positive and desirable. However there are some negative reports as well. There are about 28 source references that contain all the information that is currently out there regarding UFOs. All the others are repetition and overlap. What these works have in common is that they all take a positive view of man getting help from outer space by some type of creature that will overthrow the prophecies of the 2nd Advent. That is 28 volumes of over 200 pages each that attempt to prove that God is a liar and discount the Bible as a reliable authority. They all teach that whatever is coming from them is for mankind's benefit.

If you know much about church history, you know that there was a time when every doctrine in the Bible was hashed out and settled once and for all. The nature of God and the nature of Christ were sorted out at the Council of Nicaea in 325 A.D. and the Council at Constantinople in 381A.D. On through the centuries every doctrine has come under examination has been debated and concluded. The last issue was in 1900 when the timing of the $2^{nd}$ Advent was put under the microscope. The debate was over whether the 2nd Advent would be before or after the millennium. By 1940, everything was hammered out and the pre-millennial return of Jesus Christ was determined to be what was taught in the Scriptures. We believe that the Bible is the standard for Truth.

What standard of truth do you use? If you are still floundering around wondering about the fundamentals of the faith or if God exists then you are centuries behind. All of that has already been finalized when everything can be said about those issues has already been said. The issue now is the authority of the Word of God. Believe me when I tell you that people are trading in that authority right and left for any and everything that comes along. Are you willing to seek the Truth? What will you choose- the red pill or the blue pill? Do you want to stay in the Matrix or see what's behind the curtain? With this groundwork we head into the heart of the issue regarding UFOs.

## WHAT ARE UFOS?

Are UFOs real? If so, where did they come from and what is their agenda? What does the Bible have to say about them?

The first thing to do is to define what a UFO is. The official definition of a UFO is a reported sighting of an object or light seen in the sky, whose appearance, trajectory, actions, motions, lights and colors do not have a logical, conventional or natural explanation, and which cannot be explained, not only by the original witness, but by scientists or technical experts who tried to make a common sense identification after examining the evidence. A UFO is an "unidentified flying object." That means that something was seen flying through the air that could not be identified. There are many things that can fall into that category since there are only two criteria it must meet. The object is "flying" and it is "unidentified".

## CLASSIFICATION OF UFOs:

CE 1st kind: sighting of a UFO at close quarters

CE 2nd kind: sighting and physical evidence of the UFO

CE 3rd kind: sighting, physical evidence and all direct confrontation with the UFO occupant

CE 4th kind: abduction by aliens

CE 5th kind: contact with alien life forms through metaphysical or occultic means

CE 6th kind: injury or death from a UFO encounter

## THERE ARE 3 POSSIBLE EXPLANATIONS FOR UFOs:

1) Mistakenly identified natural phenomena

2) Hoaxes

3) Unidentifiable objects that defy the laws of physics as we know them.

It is true that many of the things reported have a natural explanation that is not identified by the observers. One example of a mistaken natural phenomenon occurred during World War II when the USS Houston fired 250 rounds at Venus while the gunnery officer kept yelling, "lengthen in your range, lengthen your range!"

It is also true that there are some hoaxes. Some folk like publicity or they just like getting a laugh on other people and they try to fool people. Some people who believe UFOs are real, manufacture evidence in an attempt to support their belief.

# FAMOUS HOAXES

- The Maury Island incident

- The Ummo affair- a decades-long series of detailed letters and documents allegedly from extraterrestrials. The documents are at least 1000 pages, and some estimate that further undiscovered documents may total nearly 4000 pages. A José Luis Jordan Peña came forward in the early nineties claiming responsibility for the phenomenon. Now, most consider there to be little reason to challenge his claims.[1]

- George Adamski- for over two decades he made various claims about his meetings with telepathic aliens from nearby planets. He claimed that there were cities, trees and snow-capped mountains on the far side of the moon.

- Ed Walters- In 1987, he allegedly perpetrated a hoax in Gulf Breeze, Florida. Walters claimed to have first seen a small UFO flying near his home and took some photographs. Walters then reported and documented a series of UFO sightings over a period of three weeks. This became known as the "Gulf Breeze UFO incident." Three years later, in 1990, after Walters had moved, the new residents discovered a model of a UFO poorly hidden in the attic that bore an undeniable resemblance to the craft in Walters' photographs. Most investigators like the forensic photo expert William G. Hyzer now consider the sightings to be a hoax.[2]

- Warren William "Billy" Smith- a popular writer who confessed to a hoax.

There are countless volumes of information regarding UFOs on the internet, but there is much disinformation about them. Most reports are uncorroborated and unreliable. Nevertheless, there remains credible evidence, involving multiple reliable witnesses and tangible evidences.

---

[1] PARANOIA – People Are Strange: Unusual UFO Cults
[2] The Gulf Breeze "UFOs"

## HISTORICAL RECORDS

In a way, the UFO phenomena is not new. It seems UFOs have been recorded at almost every age. There are records etched on stone and on Egyptian hieroglyphics. We have records of flying objects in the sky on ancient papyrus scrolls and in medieval paintings. They are evidenced on murals, pictographs, in the journal of Alexander the Great, and even in Christopher Columbus' ship's log.

**Figure 1 Egyptian Temple in Abydos depicting a helicopter (top left), submarine (top right), & a UFO (bottom of submarine).**

- In the written history of Thutmose the Third of Egypt (1480 – 1450 BC), it is recorded: "a Circle of fire appeared in the sky... Not after some time these things became more numerous in the sky than ever before. They shined more in the sky than the brightness of the sun. Powerful was the position of the fire circles... The army of Pharaoh looked with him in their midst when the circles rose higher in the sky... what happened was ordered to be written in the annals of the house of life... so that it would be remembered forever."[3]

---

[3] *Extraterrestrials*, Hitchcock & Overby, 1997 Hearthstone Publishing, pg. 23

There were sightings of flying objects in 218 BC in the Roman Empire. The accounts describe something like a shield that flew through the sky and luminous ships appeared in the heavens.

- The Roman historian Livy wrote of an unidentified object that looked like a fine altar in the sky and flew over the city of Hadria, Italy in 214 BC. Other Roman historians wrote of the appearance of unidentified flying objects all throughout the empire.

- Alexander the great wrote in his personal journal in 329 BC that his army was repeatedly harassed from the sky by two objects resembling flying "Silver Shields."

We have recapped only a small fraction of the reported sightings from ancient times. This is only a small sampling of recorded UFOs to show that these objects were seen thousands of years before Christ and all the way up to the Middle Ages. But the modern UFO era seems to have emerged since the days of World War II. Since the 1940s there have been millions of sightings. In these days, UFOs are more popular than ever. Many of these are uncorroborated and unreliable, but there are too many sightings which do not have a rational explanation to ignore.

## SOME THE AD SIGHTINGS

1. In Hungary, spherical objects shining like stars bright and polished were reported going to and fro in the sky. The year was 966 A.D.[4]

2. Two similar objects were reported in Japan and the year was 1015 A.D.

3. In a Cairo Egypt noisy flying objects were seen in 1027 A.D.

4. A large silvery disc was seen to come close to the ground in Japan in 1133 A.D.

---

[4] Anatomy, Jacques Valee

5. In 1492, just hours before landing in the New World Christopher Columbus wrote in his journal that while standing on the deck of the ship he noticed a bright object fall from the sky into the water and then exit the water and return to the skies. He and members of the crew observed other strange lights moving up and down in the distant sky.

6. Citizens of Nuremberg, Germany in 1561- witnessed a disk in the sky performing an aerial ballet.

7. Residents of Basil, Switzerland in 1566 saw a similar display.

8. Edmond Halley (of comet fame) in 1716 saw unexplained aerial objects.

9. Thousands of Californians in the 1890s reported a mysterious cigar shaped airship.

10. During World War II, American, German and Japanese pilots reported Phantom aircraft that were elliptical in shape. The term "foo fighters" was used by American fighter pilots during World War II to refer to UFOs.

11. The Battle of Los Angeles- The Battle of Los Angeles, also known as The Great Los Angeles Air Raid, is the name given by contemporary sources to the rumored enemy attack and subsequent anti-aircraft artillery barrage which took place from late February 24 to early February 25, 1942 over Los Angeles, California.[5&6] The incident occurred less than three months after the United States entered World War II as a result of the Japanese Imperial Navy's attack on Pearl Harbor, and one day after the Bombardment of Ellwood on February 23.

---

[5] Caughey, John; Caughey, LaRee (1977). Los Angeles: biography of a city. University of California Press.
[6] Farley, John E. (1998). Earthquake fears, predictions, and preparations in mid-America. Southern Illinois University Press. ISBN 9780809322015. Retrieved May 17, 2010.

**Figure 2**

*Los Angeles Times*, February 26, 1942. The photo above is the only known photograph taken of the Battle of Los Angeles. It is said however that the photo was heavily modified prior to publication. We may never know.

12. Ken Arnold- In 1947, the term "flying saucer" came into being when Ken Arnold reported seeing 9 "flying saucers" near Mt. Ranier, Washington, traveling at speeds well beyond the capability of any conventional aircraft at the time. That incident received international coverage and started the modern-day UFO movement.

**Figure 3 This shows the report Kenneth Arnold filed in 1947 about his UFO sighting.**

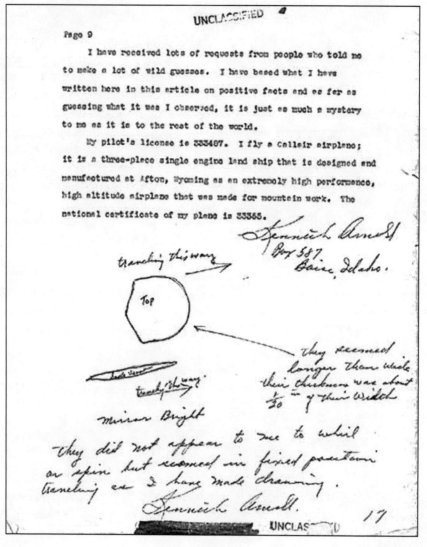

13. The Roswell Incident- An object is reported to have crashed near Roswell, New Mexico on July 6, 1947 with 4 occupants: 3 dead, 1 alive. The U.S. Army quickly sealed off the area and confiscated all the items. Then they released the famous "weather balloon" story. However, many believed this was a major cover-up due to researcher David Rudiak who used a digital photo scanner to enlarge and enhance the words written on a communiqué held by Gen. Ramey during the second press conference on July 8, 1947. He was able to identify two key phrases: "the victims of the wreck" and "in the 'disk' they will ship." The evidence for the Roswell incident is overwhelming.

14. A mass sighting occurred in the skies over Indianapolis, Indiana on July 13, 1952. A huge oval shaped craft was spotted moving very rapidly over the city. The object was visible to thousands of spectators who immediately jammed police switchboards, newspaper offices and radio stations. At the exact same time, Air Force radar personnel have locked in on a highflying craft matching the size and speed of the object seen by thousands of citizens in Indianapolis. Further, pilots from Eastern Airlines, American Airlines, and the U.S.A.F. all testified they made visual contact with the craft as it traveled over the city at a phenomenal rate of speed.

15. The mysterious Phoenix "fly-by" on March 13, 1997- A mass sighting seen by multiple witnesses and filmed over the skies of Phoenix, Arizona. However, it was not reported in the national media until June 18, 1997, where it appeared on the front page of USA Today. They had been plotted on multiple radars simultaneously and had left radiation and chemical alterations behind. Why did the media delay in reporting this event?

16. Credible accounts given by numerous military officers, commercial pilots, airport radar controllers and even astronauts.

## TESTIMONY OF THE ASTRONAUTS

- Astronaut Gordon Cooper: He claims to have chased a UFO in 1951 while he was a fighter pilot in Germany. While flying his F-86, Cooper saw what he described as "an armada of flying saucers." Cooper says he and others chased the saucers but were unable to catch them. They could not get close enough to get much detail other than that they were metallic and saucer-shaped. And again on, May 15, 1963, during the 22nd orbit of the Mercury capsule: Cooper saw a green UFO which was also tracked by Muchea's radar. Over 200 people at the tracking station watched in amazement as the object approached Cooper's module and then sped off into space. Later in a letter to the UN, Cooper stated: "I believe that these extraterrestrial vehicles and their crews are visiting this planet from other planets which are obviously a little more technologically advanced than we are here on earth."

- Walter Schirra Mercury 8, 1962: He reported a UFO orbiting his Mercury 8 space capsule and was the first to use the code name "Santa Claus" to indicate UFOs near the space capsules. Confirmed by Maurice Chatelain, Chief, NASA Communications Systems, 1979.

- Ed White & James McDivitt Gemini: In 1965 Gemini astronauts Ed White and James McDivitt made visual contact with the UFO and took several minutes of film footage as they were orbiting Earth. NASA estimates that the UFO was traveling in excess of 7000 mph. It was disc-like in shape and circled the orbiting capsule. NASA has never released the White/McDivitt film.

- James Lovell & Frank Borman Gemini 7, December 1965: Second orbit of a 14-day flight, the crew saw a UFO. Gemini control presumed it was the final stage of their own Titan Booster. They indicated that they had both the booster and the UFO in sight.

- Neil Armstrong & Edwin "Buzz" Aldrin- Apollo 11, July 21, 1969: Both apparently claimed to have seen unusual lights in a crater near their lunar landing module. According to both astronauts, there were other spacecraft there with two large objects they were watching. The following account was not only picked up by a ham operator on a public bypass channel, but was confirmed by the former chief of NASA communications, Maurice Chatelain. According to Chatelain, Armstrong had reported seeing two UFOs on the outer rim of a lunar crater. Chatelain was in the control room during many of the Mercury, Gemini and Apollo flights during the 60s and 70s. As an engineer, he secured 11 patents and held senior positions for Ryan electronics in North American aviation in the 50s and 60s.

Mission control: "what there?... Mission control calling Apollo 11...

Apollo 11: "these things are huge, sir... enormous... oh God, you wouldn't believe it! I'm telling you there are other spacecraft out there... lined up on the far side of the crater edge... there on the moon watching us..."

- In 1978, the Russian Salyut 6 orbiting spacecraft reported a formation of UFOs which trailed them closely for three complete orbits around the globe. One of the cosmonauts filmed 20 minutes of the encounter and a second took still shots. NASA stated that it is the best footage ever filmed of UFOs.

- John Blaha, Commander of Discovery Space Shuttle: Transmission, March 24, 1989 (Amateur radio intercept of private channel): "Houston, this is Discovery." "We still have the alien spacecraft under observation."

- In September 1991, the crew of the Space Shuttle Discovery videoed a clear shot of an unidentified object traveling near Discovery.

- Ed Mitchell, Apollo 14 April 1996 (Dateline, NBC): "NASA is covering up what really happened at Roswell, New Mexico."

This is only a small partial list of the documented cases. There is just too much information to list in a single volume like this.

There was a day when the topic of UFOs was not considered to be one for serious discussion among rational people. Today men and women with military and scientific backgrounds talk openly about the subject. Even with all the sightings by multiple witnesses, confirmation by radar and the like, UFOs continue to remain a mystery. Wernher von Braun, the father of modern rocketry said, "It is as impossible to confirm their existence in the present as it will be to deny their existence in the future."

There are some pretty good reasons for being skeptical. Take the 1938 War of the Worlds radio broadcast. Orson Wells was doing this bit for radio that over 6 million people heard. 1.2 million of them, missing the introduction to the program, thought it was the real thing. We know that created a widespread panic among the American people and some committed suicide because of the fear it sparked. They did not realize that was Mr. Wells was only telling a story.

First, 90 to 95% of all UFO cases are eventually solved. The majority of the cases are astronomical sources that deceive the witnesses. This would include stars and planets, aircraft lights, meteor showers and satellites. Some witnesses are seeing natural phenomena such as plasma discharges, the sun reflecting through atmospheric ice crystals and the like. And then there are the hoaxes. It is the remaining 5-10% of sightings that are looking for an explanation.

It's this small percentage of sightings that go unexplained every year and it is these sightings that draw our attention. These events are just a few of the documented sources on UFOs. If you want to know the others, there are over 6,000 professional publications in English, 2200 Foreign publications, 1350 UFO-related periodicals, 700 books on the early UFO history, and 300 books prior to 1650! This may also play a role in the widespread belief. Did you know that 57% of Americans believe in UFOs and 15% say they have seen one? 3-5% claim to have had an abduction experience.

Edward J. Reppelt, one-time head of the Air Force Project blue book had this to say about proving the existence of UFOs.

"What constitutes proof? Does a UFO have to land at the entrance to the Pentagon, near the joint Chief of Staff's offices? Or is it proof if a ground radar station detects a UFO, sends a jet to intercept it, the jet pilot sees it, and it locks on with its radar? Is it proof when a jet pilot fires at the UFO and sticks to his story even under the threat of court martial?"

UFOs are witnessed by dozens, hundreds and even thousands of people at the same time. The debate over whether or not UFOs exist may be summed up best by a point found written on the bathroom wall at the White Sands missile Range in New Mexico:

I saw a disc up in the air,

A silver disc that wasn't there,

Two more weren't there again today,

Oh, I wish they would go away!"

> "I am going to tell you that UFOs are for real.
>
> I am an eyewitness to one."

## SHAMROCK TEXAS SIGHTING

I am going to tell you that UFOs are for real. I am an eyewitness to one. As a seventeen year old teenager, 3 of my friends & I were sitting atop a high bluff in the Texas Panhandle on a clear, starry night in the summer of 1988. It was about 11:30 pm and we decided to call it a night and return home. As we started back down the bluff towards our pickup, two of us immediately spotted a strange "red light" floating in the sky just northeast of our position. It was traveling very slow and heading in a southwest direction. But there was something different about it. My friend Mark & I noticed there were no flashing lights/strobes that would be normal for an aircraft. In addition, there was no noise associated with it. It was completely silent as it traveled. As the four of us ran across the dirt road behind us to the barb-wired fence to try and identify the flying object, it came to a sudden mid-air stop. We watched it for a minute or two hover in a stationary position when it started to display erratic and bizarre behavior. It began maneuvering with extreme acceleration performing incredible acrobatic feats with acute turns across the sky! I knew that this was completely impossible for any normal aircraft to perform! We were witnessing a UFO! TJ, Mark, Shawn and I did not say a single word although I reached down and pinched myself on the forearm to see if I was dreaming. With our eyes wide open and glued to the object, there was total silence among us. It was not a dream at all!

After this impossible aerobatic display, it suddenly began to "hover" again in a fixed position. I had just witnessed a grand display. It was indeed a UFO! After several more minutes, the object began to slowly "float" away from us and then vanished in the dark night sky.

# THE GLEN ROSE/STEPHENVILLE SIGHTING

As recent as 2008, there was a sighting between Glen Rose and Stephenville, Texas. Although I was not a witness to this event, I was driving in that same location some 15-20 minutes before the sighting occurred. It was a beautiful late afternoon so I took this scenic route to watch the sunset. Just hours later, I began to hear local reports by the town's residents. They were astounded over reported sightings of what they believe was a UFO! Apparently dozens witnessed this event including two primary witnesses; a county constable named Lee Roy Gaitan and a local pilot named Steve Allen with 30 years of flight experience. Both insist they saw this UFO January 8, 2008.

In a personal interview with Steve Allen[7], he reported that the UFO was completely silent. The lights spanned about a mile long and a half mile wide. Mr. Allen believes the lights were not from a normal aircraft and were more like strobe lights. He described the lights reconfiguring themselves from a single horizontal line into two sets of vertical lights then bursting into two "white flames." John Keel, a UFO researcher, believes that color systems may be associated with UFO sightings. He suggests that:

"UFOs and their occupants move into our spatial and time [domain] they slow down, as it were, from higher frequencies, passing progressively through red, ultraviolet, violet, bluish green, and then, if they stabilize within our dimensions, they become a glaring white [light] as they radiate energy on all frequencies. With radical maneuverings at high speeds, frequencies altered, and so the colors also change. Keel shows that in the majority of landing reports the UFO's were said to have turned orange or red before they descended, then solidified when they settled to the ground and so the light would dim or go out altogether. When they took off, they again began to glow red, and it would depend on their subsequent movements as to the colors seen by the witnesses"[8].

---

[7] Personal Interview with Steve Allen on April 13, 2012
[8] Wilson, C. UFO's & Their Mission Impossible, Signet, 1974, pp 159-160

Mr. Allen witnessed the UFO travel at a high rate of speed being chased a few minutes later by F-16s! In a report released under the Freedom of Information Act, the FAA had clocked this UFO on their radar traveling at some 1,800 mph! Carswell Air Force Base in Ft. Worth initially denied any F-16s in that area this particular night. However, a man I talked with told me he had processed the paperwork for those F-16s on this particular night. Sometime later, Carswell Air Force did claim to have conducted "training exercises." But, as in any attempted cover-up, as we say in Texas, they were a day late and a dollar short. By then it was too late. Several of the original witnesses including Mr. Allen and the county constable told their story on Larry King Live. Both the History Channel and Discovery Channel along with many radio talk shows have featured this event. The Glen Rose/Stephenville sighting has been listed #3 in the top 10 UFO sightings in the world!

## THE SUTTON FAMILY CASE

Also known as the Kelly-Hopkinsville encounter, this is a well-known event in UFO history. It is considered to be an authentic close encounter of the third kind. The event occurred near the towns of Kelly and Hopkinsville, Kentucky beginning on the evening of August 21, 1955. Eleven eyewitnesses claimed that for several hours that evening and early morning, they repeatedly saw five silvery creatures about three feet tall which appeared to be glowing and floating above the ground.

The Sutton family was entertaining a friend, Billy Ray Taylor, at their farm house. When Taylor had stepped outside to get a drink of water at about 7.00 p.m., he observed strange lights in the sky to the west. He excitedly told the others about the "flying saucer" sighting but no one believed him. The others simply though he had seen a vivid "shooting star." At about 8.00 p.m., the family dog began barking loudly and then hid under the house where it stayed. Billy Ray Taylor and Elmer "Lucky" Sutton then went back outside and witnessed a strange creature emerging from the nearby trees.

The creature was described as "a luminous, three-and-a-half-foot-tall being with an oversized head, big, floppy, pointed ears, glowing eyes, and hands with talons at their ends. The figure, either made of or simply dressed in silvery metal, had its hands raised."[9]

When the creature approached within about 20 feet of the Taylor home, the men took their guns and began shooting at it, one using a shotgun, the other man using a .22 rifle. The creature, they said, then flipped over and fled into the darkness. They were sure that they had wounded the creature, so Lucky and Billy Ray set out to look for it. As the men were stepping from the porch, "a taloned-hand reached and touched his hair from above."[10] They shot at the creature again as it was perched on an awning over the porch and it was knocked from the roof. Within minutes, Lucky's brother J.C. Sutton said that he saw the same

[9] Clark, Jerome (1993). *Unexplained! 347 Strange Sightings, Incredible Occurrences, and Puzzling Physical Phenomena.* Detroit: Visible Ink Press.

type creature peer into a window in the home. Both J.C. and Billy Ray shot at it, whereupon it too flipped over and fled.

Over the next several hours, the family claimed that the creatures repeatedly approached their home, whereby they continued to shoot at them each time they did. On one occasion, one of the family shot one of the creatures at point blank range. They said the sound resembled bullets striking a metal bucket. The floating creatures' legs seemed to be atrophied and nearly useless. They appeared to propel themselves with a curious hip-swaying motion, steering with their arms. Apparently, if the creatures were in a tree or on the roof when hit by gunfire, they would just float away and not fall to the ground.

Around 11.00 p.m., the Taylor-Sutton crew decided to flee their home in automobiles. Thirty minutes later they arrived at the Hopkinsville police station. Police Chief Russell Greenwell said the witnesses were frightened by something "beyond reason, not ordinary." He also said that these were not the sort of people who normally ran to the police; that something frightened them; something beyond their comprehension."[11] A police officer with medical training determined that Billy Ray's pulse rate was more than twice normal. At about that same time, a

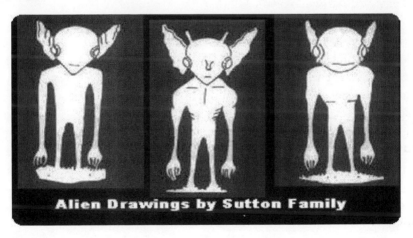

**Alien Drawings by Sutton Family**

---

[11] Ibid

state highway trooper near Kelly independently reported some unusual "meteors" flying overhead "with a sound like artillery fire."

Several police officers accompanied the Taylor-Suttons back to their home and saw many bullet holes and empty shell casings. They further discovered what looked like an odd luminous area along a fence where one of the creatures had been shot, and, in the woods beyond, another area with luminous green light whose source could not be determined immediately. No samples were taken for further analysis. Police left at about 2:15 a.m., but then not long afterwards, the Sutton family claims that the creatures returned. Billy Ray fired upon them once more, shattering a window. The last of the creatures was allegedly sighted at about 4:45 a.m. the next morning on August 22.

Later on the 22nd, Andrew "Bud" Ledwith of WHOP radio interviewed the seven adult witnesses in two different groups. Ledwith had worked as a professional artist, and sketched the creatures based on the witnesses' descriptions. Their descriptions were generally consistent, though the female witnesses insisted that the creatures had a somewhat husker build than the male witnesses remembered, and Billy Ray Taylor was alone in insisting that the beings had antennae.

The farm became a tourist attraction for a brief period but eventually the Suttons refused all visitors and refused to discuss the incident any further. Project Blue Book, the official UFO investigation office, never officially investigated the case, although a file has been kept on it. It is unclear why they did not investigate one of the most important close encounters of the 3rd kind ever reported.

There is something out there. In spite of the natural phenomena, the misidentifications and the hoaxes, there is something out there. Orson Welles summed up the thoughts of many when he said, "The discovery of just one bacteria on Mars or any other body of the solar system would indicate that the whole chain of evolution is at work everywhere... the more we studied the evidence that is being assembled from all over the earth, the more inescapable the conclusion becomes that man should prepare himself for the greatest event in human history - the realization that we are about to contact or be contacted by you being from another universe."

*Chapter 2*

# The Bible & UFOs

I t almost goes without saying that there are creatures mentioned in the Bible that defy imagination. That makes the Bible a "fertile field" for those who want to impose their own interpretation on the Scriptures, making their agenda the Bible's agenda.

There have been those on the outer fringes of Ufology that have proposed that Jesus Himself worked His miracles by using UFO crafts. For example, when the gospels record that Jesus took just a few loaves and fishes and fed thousands, some explain the miracle by claiming that UFO's quietly hovered overhead of the unsuspecting crowd and lowered food down to Jesus, who then fed the multitudes. Even the parting of the Red Sea was an event that some have claimed that involved the use of alien spacecraft and technologies. Von Daniken claims that the vision of Ezekiel was a spacecraft and that God is an ancient astronaut! He himself has stated that the ancient astronaut theory came to him on an astral trip and that he knows himself to be a reincarnated ancient astronaut![12]

Perhaps the most referred to scripture which is used to place the Bible's blessing on the existence of UFOs is in the book of Ezekiel. As proof of his Ancient Astronaut Theory, Eric Von Daniken cited the writings of Ezekiel! Let's take a look at the two most referenced passages; Ezekiel 1 and Ezekiel 10.

---

[12] Steiger,B. The Fellowship, Ivy Books, p. 64

**Ezekiel 1:4 (KJV)**
4 And I looked, and, behold, a whirlwind came out of the north, a great cloud, and a fire infolding itself, and a brightness was about it, and out of the midst thereof as the colour of amber, out of the midst of the fire.

**Ezekiel 1:16-18 (KJV)**
16 **The appearance of the wheels** and their work was like unto the colour of a beryl: and they four had one likeness: and their appearance and their work was as it were **a wheel in the middle of a wheel**.
17 When they went, they went upon their four sides: and they turned not when they went.
18 As for their rings, they were so high that they were dreadful; and their rings were full of eyes round about them four.

**Ezekiel 10:10-11 (KJV)**
10 And as for their appearances, they four had one likeness, as if **a wheel had been in the midst of a wheel.**
11 When they went, they went upon their four sides; they turned not as they went, but to the place whither the head looked they followed it; they turned not as they went.

For many, all they needed to see was the phrase, "a wheel in the midst of a wheel." That supposedly "proves" the Bible describing a UFO. Unfortunately, the most identifying parts of the passages are overlooked by this kind of "private interpretation." The Bible clearly identifies some creatures that it identifies as Cherubim in both of these chapters. These are not machines with occupants inside them, but living creatures. Granted, the likes of these creatures have never been seen by men on earth, but they are part of the angelic host, charged with the transport of the very throne of God. I admit that an accurate artistic portrayal of these creatures would be fantastic, to say the least. But the Bible is not describing flying saucers when it describes these cherubim. Let's read the full text and you will see what I mean.

**Ezekiel 1:4-14 (KJV)**
4 And I looked, and, behold, a whirlwind came out of the north, a great cloud, and a fire infolding itself, and a brightness was

about it, and out of the midst thereof as the colour of amber, out of the midst of the fire.

⁵ Also out of the midst thereof *came* the likeness of **four living creatures**. And **this *was* their appearance**; they had the likeness of a man.

⁶ And every one had four faces, and every one had four wings.

⁷ And their feet *were* straight feet; and the sole of their feet *was* like the sole of a calf's foot: and they sparkled like the colour of burnished brass.

⁸ And *they had* the hands of a man under their wings on their four sides; and they four had their faces and their wings.

⁹ Their wings *were* joined one to another; they turned not when they went; they went every one straight forward.

¹⁰ As for the likeness of their faces, they four had the face of a man, and the face of a lion, on the right side: and they four had the face of an ox on the left side; they four also had the face of an eagle.

¹¹ Thus *were* their faces: and their wings *were* stretched upward; two *wings* of every one *were* joined one to another, and two covered their bodies.

¹² And they went every one straight forward: whither the spirit was to go, they went; *and* they turned not when they went.

¹³ As for the likeness of the living creatures, their appearance *was* like burning coals of fire, *and* like the appearance of lamps: it went up and down among the living creatures; and the fire was bright, and out of the fire went forth lightning.

¹⁴ And the living creatures ran and returned as the appearance of a flash of lightning.

Verse 4 says declares these are "four living creatures." Then, in verse 5, it declares "this was their appearance." What follows is a description of the living creatures, not a mechanical flying machine. These creatures do fly, but you should not confuse them with a UFO any more than you would confuse any other animal that can fly with an alien spacecraft.

They have "wings" and "hands" and "faces." Yes, there is the appearance of "lamps" of fire that "go up and down among the creatures" and "out of the fire went forth lightening." But notice that Ezekiel is not confused into thinking he is observing some "light show" or a display of "lightening." He demonstrates clearly that the "lamps of fire" are "among the creatures." That is, when you see these, you would not just be seeing the lamps. Now, we need to read further in Ezekiel 1. I realize this is a lengthy passage, but we include it here because if all we do is mention the reference, most people will not go look it up. Therefore, we include it for convenience sake.

> These "wheels" are not the saucers or flying discs that many claim to have seen.

### Ezekiel 1:15-25 (KJV)
15 Now as I beheld the living creatures, behold one wheel upon the earth by the living creatures, with his four faces.
16 The appearance of the wheels and their work was like unto the colour of a beryl: and they four had one likeness: and their appearance and their work was as it were a wheel in the middle of a wheel.
17 When they went, they went upon their four sides: and they turned not when they went.
18 As for their rings, they were so high that they were dreadful; and their rings were full of eyes round about them four.
19 And when the living creatures went, the wheels went by them: and when the living creatures were lifted up from the earth, the wheels were lifted up.
20 Whithersoever the spirit was to go, they went, thither was their spirit to go; and the wheels were lifted up over against them: for the spirit of the living creature was in the wheels.
21 When those went, these went; and when those stood, these stood; and when those were lifted up from the earth, the wheels were lifted up over against them: for the spirit of the living creature was in the wheels.
22 And the likeness of the firmament upon the heads of the living creature was as the colour of the terrible crystal, stretched forth over their heads above.
23 And under the firmament were their wings straight, the one toward the other: every one had two, which covered on this side, and every one had two, which covered on that side, their bodies.

24 And when they went, I heard the noise of their wings, like the noise of great waters, as the voice of the Almighty, the voice of speech, as the noise of an host: when they stood, they let down their wings.

25 And there was a voice from the firmament that was over their heads, when they stood, and had let down their wings.

It is evident that the "wheels" are not the only thing in view. Ezekiel sees that they are "lifted up over against the creatures." Have you ever heard of a UFO that was lifted up against a creature? These "wheels" are not the saucers or flying discs that many claim to have seen. Finally, I would give you just a small reference in Ezekiel 10, for it is here that we see the creatures identified for exactly what they are; cherubim.

### Ezekiel 10:1-16 (KJV)

1 Then I looked, and, behold, in the firmament that was above the head of the **cherubims** there appeared over them as it were a sapphire stone, as the appearance of the likeness of a throne.

3 Now **the cherubims** stood on the right side of the house, when the man went in; and the cloud filled the inner court.

4 Then the glory of the LORD went up from the cherub, and stood over the threshold of the house; and the house was filled with the cloud, and the court was full of the brightness of the LORD'S glory.

5 And the sound of **the cherubims' wings** was heard even to the outer court, as the voice of the Almighty God when he speaketh.

6 And it came to pass, that when he had commanded the man clothed with linen, saying, Take fire from between the wheels, from between the cherubims; then he went in, and stood beside the wheels.

7 And one cherub stretched forth his hand from between the cherubims unto **the fire that was between the cherubims,** and took thereof, and put it into the hands of him that was clothed with linen: who took it, and went out.

[8] And there appeared in the cherubims the form of a man's hand under their wings.

[9] And when I looked, behold **the four wheels by the cherubims, one wheel by one cherub,** and **another wheel by**

**another cherub**: and the appearance of the wheels *was* as the colour of a beryl stone.

[10] And *as for* their appearances, they four had one likeness, as if **a wheel had been in the midst of a wheel**.

14 And every one had four faces: the first face was the face of a cherub, and the second face was the face of a man, and the third the face of a lion, and the fourth the face of an eagle.

15 And the **cherubims** were lifted up. This is the living creature that I saw by the river of Chebar.

16 And **when the cherubims went, the wheels went by them**: and when the cherubims lifted up their wings to mount up from the earth, the same wheels also turned not from beside them.

For those of you who are wondering what is going on in these chapters, let me give you the salient points of the action. All the way back to Leviticus 26, God predicted the entirely of Israel's future. As you read that chapter you will find 5 courses of judgment set forth, each one progressively worse than the one before. The 5th and final course begins the judgment of God against His people in their being "spewed out of the land" of promise.[13] Historically, that judgment was carried out (on the southern kingdom of Judah) by king Nebuchadnezzar and the Babylonians.

Prior to their being led away captive out of the land, Ezekiel is given a vision of the LORD, seated upon His throne and carried by the cherubim, leaving the land of Israel. The movement is progressive: He moves from the temple, to the outer court, to the edge of the city (Jerusalem), to the borders of the land of Israel and finally from off the earth entirely. That is the vision you are given to see in these chapters. Of course, there is much more to see about this, but then, that is not the focus of this book.

We find another reference to the cherubs in 2 Samuel. The context of the passage is during the LORD's day of wrath, when "the earth shook," (vs. 8) and the "foundations of heaven moved," (vs. 8) and the LORD "thundered from heaven" (vs. 14) at His 2nd Advent when He

---

[13] See Lev. 18:28; 20:22

returns, according to the Davidic Covenant, to function as Israel's Avenger! At that time, He will "ride upon a cherub!" Those who see Him, will not confuse Him with riding a flying saucer!

### 2 Samuel 22:7-16 (KJV)

7 In my distress I called upon the LORD, and cried to my God: and he did hear my voice out of his temple, and my cry did enter into his ears.

[8] Then **the earth shook and trembled**; the **foundations of heaven moved** and shook, because he was wroth.

[9] There went up a smoke out of his nostrils, and fire out of his mouth devoured: coals were kindled by it.

[10] He bowed the heavens also, and came down; and darkness *was* under his feet.

[11] And **he rode upon a cherub, and did fly**: and he was seen upon the wings of the wind.

[12] And he made darkness pavilions round about him, dark waters, *and* thick clouds of the skies.

[13] Through the brightness before him were coals of fire kindled.

[14] **The LORD thundered from heaven**, and the most High uttered his voice.

[15] And he sent out arrows, and scattered them; lightning, and discomfited them.

[16] And the channels of the sea appeared, the foundations of the world were discovered, at the rebuking of the LORD, at the blast of the breath of his nostrils.

### Psalms 18:10-15 (KJV)

10 And **he rode upon a cherub**, and did fly: yea, he did fly upon the wings of the wind.

11 He made darkness his secret place; his pavilion round about him were dark waters and thick clouds of the skies.

12 At the brightness that was before him his thick clouds passed, hail stones and coals of fire.

13 The LORD also thundered in the heavens, and the Highest gave his voice; hail stones and coals of fire.

14 Yea, he sent out his arrows, and scattered them; and he shot out lightnings, and discomfited them.

15 Then the channels of waters were seen, and the foundations

of the world were discovered at thy rebuke, O LORD, at the blast of the breath of thy nostrils.

It is not my intention to write a treatise on these creatures, but only to show that "their appearance" is not to be confused with a UFO craft. We will discuss these Cherubim and how they fit into the picture in the next chapter. As we have shown here, both 2nd Samuel and Psalm 18 confirm that what we have been looking with regard to "chariot of the LORD" and the cherubim in Ezekiel 1 (and Ezekiel 10) is the chariot of the Lord which will make an appearance at the Second Advent. Many people, regarding the "wheel within a wheel" start thinking of a UFO description in Ezekiel, and I will grant you that it is a strange appearance with 4 cherubim with four faces and four wings with four wheels carrying a firmament with a throne that the Lord will be seated on!

Remember we are talking about unidentified flying objects, not flying saucers, not space ships; but things that are not identified that fly. People automatically assume that when you say UFO, you are saying flying saucer. They also assume the Bible doesn't have any UFOs. But let me take you over to the book of Zechariah, who is a 5th cycle prophet.[14] In Zechariah, who is writing about the things which will be happening in the last days of Israel's program, we find something that could definitely be called an unidentified flying object.

## THE FLYING ROLL

### Zechariah 5:1-11 (KJV)
1 Then I turned, and lifted up mine eyes, and looked, and behold **a flying roll**.
2 And he said unto me, What seest thou? And I answered, I see a flying roll; the length thereof *is* twenty cubits, and the breadth thereof ten cubits.
3 Then said he unto me, This *is* the curse that goeth forth over the face of the whole earth: for every one that stealeth shall be

---

[14] For more info on this go to www.graceage.org & the Millennium Bible Institute's School of Eschatology.

cut off *as* on this side according to it; and every one that sweareth shall be cut off *as* on that side according to it.

⁴ I will bring it forth, saith the LORD of hosts, and it shall enter into the house of the thief, and into the house of him that sweareth falsely by my name: and it shall remain in the midst of his house, and shall consume it with the timber thereof and the stones thereof.

⁵ Then the angel that talked with me went forth, and said unto me, Lift up now thine eyes, and see what *is* this that goeth forth.

⁶ And I said, What *is* it? And he said, This *is* an ephah that goeth forth. He said moreover, This *is* their resemblance through all the earth.

⁷ And, behold, there was lifted up a talent of lead: and this *is* a woman that sitteth in the midst of the ephah.

⁸ And he said, This *is* wickedness. And he cast it into the midst of the ephah; and he cast the weight of lead upon the mouth thereof.

⁹ Then lifted I up mine eyes, and looked, and, behold, there came out two women, and the wind *was* in their wings; for they had wings like the wings of a stork: and they lifted up the ephah between the earth and the heaven.

¹⁰ Then said I to the angel that talked with me, Whither do these bear the ephah?

¹¹ And he said unto me, To build it an house in the land of Shinar: and it shall be established, and set there upon her own base.

Now, you might say, well, this thing flies, but it not unidentified; it is a scroll. Have you ever seen a flying scroll that is 20 cubits long (30') and 10 cubits wide (15')? Let your eyes skip down to verse 3 and read that this "scroll" is a "curse." Have you ever seen a flying "curse" that is 30 feet long? If you did, do you think you could identify it?

Look at vv. 3-4 and see where it goes. It goes "over the face of the whole earth" (Vs. 3). It goes into people's houses (Vs. 4). Now, the doctrine of this is pretty amazing, because it isn't just anybody's house that this thing goes into, and where it goes has to do with what God is doing on the earth in the day of the LORD. But notice what it does to those houses – it destroys them (Vs. 4).

But we aren't through with the bizarre just yet. Take a look down in vs. 7 where you see an ephah (think of a basket) with a woman sitting in the midst of it. Wickedness is cast into the ephah and then a lid of lead is put on top to seal it in the basket with the woman. And then, as if all this were not enough, 2 women, with wings like storks (unclean birds) fly off with the ephah. The angel says, "This is wickedness." But here is my point; if you saw this flying through the air, this basket with winged women carrying it, what would you say it was? You would probably wonder what it was you did see – which would make this an "unidentified flying object." Any object that cannot be described by normal identification can correctly be classified as a "UFO."

You can write these things off if you want to, but the Bible doesn't tell you about this just to entertain you. Now let's look at the next reference in 2 Samuel 5. The context is the time when David was anointed king over Israel. The Philistines and Israel are set for battle and David has already defeated them once. Now, the Philistines come up a second time and God gives David instructions as to how to engage the enemy.

> **2 Samuel 5:23-24 (KJV)**
> 23 And when David enquired of the LORD, he said, Thou shalt not go up; but fetch a compass behind them, and come upon them over against the mulberry trees.
> <sup>24</sup> And let it be, when thou hearest **the sound of a going in the tops of the mulberry trees,** that then thou shalt bestir thyself: for then shall the LORD go out before thee, to smite the host of the Philistines.

What I'm really after here is the "sound of a going in the tops of the mulberry trees." You say, it is just referring to the wind blowing. Then why didn't it say that? The Bible does talk about "wind," after all. In fact, over 100 times! For example, Job 1:19.

> **Job 1:19 (KJV)**
> 19 And, behold, there came a great wind from the wilderness, and smote the four corners of the house, and it fell upon the young men, and they are dead; and I only am escaped alone to tell thee.

Did you notice that it did not say there came a great "sound of a going in the tops of the trees?" It just said "wind." But here is my point; I see a difference between "hearing the wind blow" and hearing the sound of "something going in the tops of the trees." Did you ever hear the wind blow and look up to see if something was moving in the trees – or did you just know it was the wind? You knew it was the wind. Well, if I'm right, then again, we have something "going in the tops of the trees" (indicating it is flying) and that thing that is *going* is "unidentified." That would technically be a UFO. Again, this is not a flying saucer or an alien spacecraft, but something that is perceived to be flying without being able to identify it.

But let's talk about another part of the UFO phenomena; those who claim to be a part of it. Do you recall the Heaven's Gate group that wound up committing suicide? Back when I was working in a church in Baton Rouge, Louisiana, one of our young men (who was attending LSU) brought me a placard that had been posted on the LSU campus. It announced that part of (what we refer to as the Heaven's Gate group) was going to be at the Holiday Inn in Port Allen, which is right across the river from Baton Rouge. The placard promised that people would be shown the way to heaven via a UFO. It gave the address, the meeting room and the time.

I printed up a number of tracts titled: UFOs: Friend or Foe? Inside the tracts, I talked about the satanic deception and gave the gospel. It is my personal understanding that most of the UFO sightings are nothing to get excited about. Some of them are either natural things which are not clearly perceived or people are being dishonest, making up encounters and sightings. I believe the fakes to be the bigger group. However, I do believe that there are a few genuine sightings, encounters, etc. that cannot be explained away and for which there is sufficient evidence that suggests there is something of the supernatural involved. For those few encounters, I am firmly convinced that they are demonic in nature. And we plan to support that belief from the Scriptures in this book.

But getting back to the story, I attended the meeting, armed with my stack of tracts and a cassette recorder. I was told at the door that recordings were not permitted, and I had to give up my recorder until the meeting was over. As the meeting started, several men and a woman came out to the front and sat facing the audience. They appeared to be "glassy eyed" and "robotic" in their movements. That's the best way I can describe them. They spoke in monotone voices about carrying us to a "higher spiritual plane" in a UFO. They called this "higher spiritual plane" the "kingdom of heaven" and "the kingdom of God." After about a 25 – 30 minute presentation in which people were invited to join them by giving over all their material goods to the group, they asked if there were any questions. I raised my hand. When they called on me, I asked them how a UFO could carry anyone to a "higher spiritual plane" without addressing the issue of sin. I mentioned that "without the shedding of blood, there is no remission of sin," so how were they planning to address the problem of sin? Instead of answering me, the man said, "We perceive you are a troublemaker and we will not answer your question."

As other people began to ask questions of the panel, I was busy handing tracts out to people around me. As it turns out, there were some other Christians there and they asked for tracts to pass out as well. After a few minutes, I raised my hand again. They called on me and I asked them about the UFO carrying people to the "kingdom of heaven." I explained that according to the Bible, the kingdom of heaven was going to take place on this earth, so where is the UFO taking people? Again I got the response, "We perceive you are a troublemaker and we will not answer your question."

I waited a few more minutes and raised my hand again. This time, they would not call on me. So I moved to the other side of the room and seated myself in the middle of a crowd of people. I raised my hand and they called on me. As I began my question, I guess they recognized me and again said they would not answer my questions. A Christian lady behind me leaned up and said, "Tell me your question and I'll ask it." I gave her the question and she asked it and they refused to answer her question. With that, they cut off any further questions and dismissed the group. A number of people then stepped up to the front and began to talk with these people face to face. I also went up and asked them if they believed the Bible. They said they believed only the words of Jesus and the book of Revelation.

I challenged one of them to debate the reality of their claims in front of an open Bible, using only the words of Jesus and the book of Revelation. He took me up on it and we sat down. Our agreement was if I could prove him false, he would admit it was all a scam. If I could not, then I would join their group. So, I opened my Bible and I asked him to affirm what he had already said in the meeting, "Do you claim that you are a prophet from God?" He answered that He was. I asked him again if he believed the words of Jesus to be true. He said he did. I then turned to Luke 16:16 and quoted the words of Jesus (in red!), "Luke 16:16 The law and **the prophets were until John**: since that time the kingdom of God is preached, and every man presseth into it."

After reading the verse I said, "According to Jesus, the prophets were 'until John.' John has been gone for centuries, so on what basis are you a prophet?" I then declared him to be a false prophet. He jumped angrily from his chair and declared the debate to be over. I tried my best to expose him (and his cohorts) for the false prophet he was. But don't you know one guy actually joined their group that night. Talk about being deceived!

I did not recognize that group for who they were at the time. It was only later when the group had gained some recognition, and when they all committed suicide, did I realize it was the Heaven's Gate group I had encountered that night.

# Chapter 3

# Cherubim &

# Winged Serpents

WE talked a little about the Cherubim in the prior chapter. But who are they? They are an order of certain Angels who have a particular function concerning the throne of God. They are intelligent spirit beings who have a will & emotions. They can speak and even eat meals. They are capable of direct physical combat such as the account of the Passover in Egypt or in which 185,000 Syrians were killed in 2 Kings 19:35.

In Genesis 19:1 we see the angels in Sodom appeared as wingless males who were normal looking men in the physical.

In case you are wondering, here is the order:

1. Archangels (Michael)

2. Principalities

3. Powers

4. Virtues

5. Dominions

6. Thrones

7. Cherubim (angels with 4 wings)

8. Seraphim (angels with 6 wings)

Although this is not a study on Angels, there are some details that you should be aware of regarding the Cherubim. This will give us a vital clue later on.

A.S. Judkins/Michael McDaniel

### Ezekiel 1:4-6 (KJV)

4 And I looked, and, behold, a whirlwind came out of the north, a great cloud, and a fire infolding itself, and a brightness was about it, and out of the midst thereof as the colour of amber, out of the midst of the fire.

5 Also out of the midst thereof came the likeness of **four living creatures**. And this was their appearance; **they had the likeness of a man**.

6 **And every one had four faces, and every one had four wings**.

Cherubim have four faces: the face of a lion, an ox, a man, and an eagle. The Scripture confirms these beasts which are exactly the same in Revelation.[15]

### Revelation 4:6-7 (KJV)

6 And before the throne *there was* a sea of glass like unto crystal: and in the midst of the throne, and round about the throne, *were* four beasts full of eyes before and behind.

7 And the first beast *was* like a **lion**, and the second beast like a **calf**, and the third beast had a face as a **man**, and the fourth beast *was* like a flying **eagle**.

In Ezekiel chapter 10, we see the description of the cherubs again, but this time there is something different. It is with the absence of the calf or ox.

### Ezekiel 10:14 (KJV)

[14] And every one had four faces: the **first face** *was* the face of a **cherub**, and the **second face** *was* the face of a **man**, and the **third the face** of a **lion**, and the **fourth** the face of an **eagle**.

So here is what we have thus far regarding the Cherubim:

---

[15] These are the same living creatures of Ezekiel. John calls them beasts in Revelation.

| Ezekiel 1 | Ezekiel 10 | Revelation 4 |
|-----------|------------|--------------|
| Lion | Lion | Lion |
| **Ox** | **Cherub** | **Calf** |
| Man | Man | Man |
| Eagle | Eagle | Eagle |

Notice the face of the Cherub. It is the face of a calf (ox)! The cross reference is Ezekiel 28.

### Ezekiel 28:11-16 (KJV)

[11] Moreover the word of the LORD came unto me, saying,
[12] Son of man, take up a lamentation upon the king of Tyrus, and say unto him, Thus saith the Lord GOD; Thou sealest up the sum, full of wisdom, and perfect in beauty.
[13] *Thou* **has been in Eden the garden of God**; every precious stone *was* thy covering, the sardius, topaz, and the diamond, the beryl, the onyx, and the jasper, the sapphire, the emerald, and the carbuncle, and gold: the workmanship of thy tabrets and of thy pipes was prepared in thee in the day that thou wast created.
[14] **Thou** *art* **the anointed cherub that covereth**; and I have set thee *so*: thou wast upon the holy mountain of God; thou hast walked up and down in the midst of the stones of fire.
[15] Thou *wast* perfect in thy ways from the day that thou wast created, till iniquity was found in thee.
[16] By the multitude of thy merchandise they have filled the midst of thee with violence, and thou hast sinned: therefore I will cast thee as profane out of the mountain of God: and I will destroy thee, O covering cherub, from the midst of the stones of fire.

What is described in the text? There is a lion which represents the wild animals, a calf which represents the domesticated animals, the man representing the human race, and an eagle representing the bird class. But there is one class missing. It is the reptilian class which is represented by the serpent or dragon. Lucifer has lost his place as the "covering cherub!"

## ATTRIBUTES OF SATAN

- Satan was the anointed cherub before he fell.

- Satan is now the great red dragon.

- When he appears, he appears as an angel of light.

- He represents the reptile class which is the dragon or serpent.

- The essence of the cherub is the ox. (This is why the occult and pagan rituals worship the face of an ox. An example in history is Baal worship. They are actually worshipping the winged "cherub" and serpent "dragon" which is Satan.)

- Cherubs have wings.

This is why Genesis 3 says that the serpent is cursed above all cattle.

Now we can clearly see the 4 faces (characteristics) of Satan; the fallen cherub.

1. **The man**- Satan tempts man to keep him separated from the redemption of Christ (Matthew 4:3)

2. **The lion**- Satan is a roaring lion seeking to kill, steal, & destroy (1 Peter 5:8)

3. **The eagle**- Satan is the prince of the power of the air (Ephesians 2:2)

4. **The ox (calf)** - Satan desires worship as God. We see throughout history of different cultures people worshipping the calf! This yokes people to bondage (Isaiah 10:27)

# THE WINGED SERPENT

What we know from the Bible is that Lucifer (light-bearer) is associated with an ox, bull or calf. He is also associated with sun and fire, the serpent, the winged serpent, and the dragon. Knowing this sheds new light on the UFO phenomena, which I believe will greatly play into world events after the Rapture of the Church.

The following is a true story investigated by the Condon Committee[16] on February 13, 1968.

> It was December 3, 1967 2:10 A.M. in Ashland, Nebraska. It was a cold winter night on the outskirts of Ashland. Herbert Shirmer, a police officer, was driving his patrol car along a desolate road. Suddenly, Shirmer saw a flashing light blinking rapidly off in the distance. He thought he had better try to follow it. It settled on a distant hill. When he approached it, his car stopped and the lights went out. He was frightened as he saw some figures come out of the UFO and walk towards him! It seemed like a weird dream. Shirmer seemed to be in a trance. He could not move. He looked

---

[16] The Condon Committee was the informal name of the University of Colorado UFO Project, a group funded by the United States Air Force from 1966 to 1968 at the University of Colorado to study unidentified flying objects under the direction of physicist Edward Condon. The result of this work, formally entitled "Scientific Study of Unidentified Flying Objects", and known as the Condon Report, appeared in 1968.

at the figures and saw a strange emblem on the left side of their chests. It was a WINGED SERPENT! There was a power about these creatures that was supernatural. He could not draw his gun or move. The creatures looked him over and then returned to the UFO and it took off disappearing in the distance.

The question arises, "why a winged serpent" when there is no such thing as a snake with wings? If Herbert Shirmer did indeed see an emblem of a winged serpent, then we have a clue to reveal the mystery behind the UFO phenomena. The story is startling. The unveiling of the deceptions of an evil power that has come down through the history of the world and revolves around the legend of a winged serpent god!

The Bible mentions fiery flying serpents and the connotation is always evil.

### Isaiah 30:6 (KJV)
[6] The burden of the beasts of the south: into the land of trouble and anguish, from whence *come* the young and old lion, the viper and **fiery flying serpent**, they will carry their riches upon the shoulders of young asses, and their treasures upon the bunches of camels, to a people *that* shall not profit *them*.

In history we find the winged serpent all over the place; for example, in the grave of Seti 1 in the Valley of the Kings. We will do a cursory examination of the evidence beginning with Egypt since that is the context of the Isaiah 30 text. Why does this verse mention a winged serpent?

Let's go back to the year 1922. The place is the "Valley of the Tombs" in Egypt. Archaeologist, Howard Carter had searched for 30 years for the tomb of King Tut. At last he was sure he had found the entrance to the tomb. It was the afternoon on November 22. In front of Carter was a door, believed to be sealed for 3,300 years! Carefully, Carter chiseled at a corner of the door. His companion, Lord Carnarvon, peered over his shoulder. Bit by bit the hole widened.

Finally the hole was large enough to shine a light inside the dark tomb. Carter, with trembling hands, held a flashlight to the opening and turned it on. After Carter widened the hole, both men peered into the tomb. The flashlight revealed one of the greatest archaeological finds in history.

They saw huge headed animals covered with gold. As the light moved, it revealed life sized statues of men facing each other like sentinels before a sealed door. There were overturned chariots, glistening with gold. There was a mass of jewelry, artifacts, furniture, clothing and weapons. The men were amazed at what they saw. For centuries this tomb was in darkness. Now it treasures were to be seen by mankind and its secrets revealed once again.

As Carter and Carnarvon entered one chamber after another, they gazed upon priceless treasures. These treasures made this tomb unique. The burial chamber held the greatest treasure; the body of King Tut. He was within three coffins. The innermost casket weighed over 2000 pounds of pure gold! Carter discovered 143 gold jewels on the mummified body of the boy King. The coffins were so perfectly fitted together, a little finger could not be inserted between them. But there was something else in the tomb that was a part of one of the strangest mysteries in the history of man.

Symbols are a universal language. Where ever you go you can find the same symbols and various cultures throughout the earth. In the tomb of King Tut, symbols were everywhere. The boy King had a golden casket over his body that preserved the features of the King. On the headdress, two creatures are beautifully designed. One is a vulture, the other a serpent. Egyptologist tells us that this represents Upper and Lower Egypt. But there is more meaning to the symbols. The serpent meant the "GIVING OF LIFE" and the vulture referred to death. The Pharaoh was said to have power over life and death!

One of the golden amulets in King Tut's tomb pictures the boy King on his chariot. Behind the chariot was a snake with wings. This WINGED SERPENT was to protect the Pharaoh. Two black boxes were found in King Tut's tomb. And in these boxes, two winged serpents were housed. Beautifully made out of gold, they were significant in the belief of life after death. The Egyptians called these two winged serpents, "THE DIVINE SERPENTS" showing that they represented a protecting God.

As the many discoveries came forth from King Tut's tomb, the winged serpent was to be seen time after time in the tomb. It is a marvel how many times the winged serpent was seen throughout the art of Egypt. The sun was considered to be the GREAT LIFE GIVER in the heavens and the serpent, the LIFE GIVER on earth. The wings represent the heavenly aspect of the gods. A human head on the body of a snake with wings is sometimes found. It is seen on a golden amulet found in King Tut's tomb. In Central America, the winged serpent god has a human head on the body of a snake with wings as well, showing that these symbols are universal.

One of the greatest marvels of King Tut's tomb was his golden throne. Beautifully wrought in gold, the armrests are made of two winged serpents. Why would King Tut, the one that was worshiped as the son of the sun god and the life giver, have two winged serpents on his golden throne? For years our history books told the story of King Tut, dying of tuberculosis when he was about 18 years old. Recently, scientists discovered that he was actually murdered and his murderer's name was "AY".

The ironic thing about this murder is that the winged serpents on either side of King Tut were to act as protectors for the King! They were like covering Angels.

It is a strange fact that man has believed a lie ever since the fall in the Garden of Eden. The same lies have echoed down through the history of the world and people still believe these same lies. They are, "DID GOD SAY"? and "YE SHALL NOT SURELY DIE." (Genesis 3:1,4). The first questioned God's authority. The second was a lie posed as a statement of fact.

Snakes with wings are found in many forms in Egyptian art. They were painted on caskets of the Kings and Queens. Winged serpents were not only painted on caskets, the body of the serpent extended the full length of the casket. There are tombs in central Egypt that have pairs of winged serpents on the opposite walls. The serpent represented the life giver and the body moving up and down represented the immortality of the soul.

Dragons are also seen in the art of the world. Ancient Egypt was no exception. Egyptian artists painted winged serpents with legs and called them dragons. They are not as numerous as winged serpents or serpents in general, yet they can be seen in the art of Egypt. Once again the question can be asked, "Why?"

Maya legends tell us that the winged serpent god came from an unknown country of the rising Sun in a white robe, and he wore a beard. He was a lawgiver and taught the arts and sciences. When this god fulfilled his mission, he returned to the sea, preaching and teaching on the way, and boarded a ship which took him to the morning star. This winged serpent god promised to return. The legend was remembered and when Hernando Cortez, the Spanish Conquistador, landed in Mexico in 1519, he was thought to be the winged serpent god in his reincarnated state!

In the days of Cortez and Pizarro, Spanish ships carried a blood red Maltese cross; the great sun symbol. The sun god was thought to be the sky god by many cultures around the world. Mankind has always looked to the skies for the home of its gods and winged deities represented the heavenly aspect of the gods. You can easily see why Montezuma, the Aztec King, was confused and thought that the Spaniards were the returning winged serpent god of the sun.

A great ship glides towards the shore. Its massive sails with crosses of red seemed to have a spell on the natives. As the ship comes closer, they wonder if this is the winged serpent god that their legends said would come from the east. The ship anchored in the bay. Hernando Cortez had sailed from Cuba to conquer Mexico for Spain. He and his men came ashore in small boats. The natives wondered what kind of beings were coming ashore. They saw that

> Once again the Dragon and Winged Serpent are associated together.

they were white men with clothing and the armor glistening in the sun. Surely this was the return of the great White god they thought. Eventually Cortez and his men were brought before Montezuma; Lord of many kings. It was believed that his equal was not known in the entire world. Montezuma knew the legend of the winged serpent god that would return to the earth as the great white god.

As Cortez and his men came ashore they were prepared for battle, but instead the natives bowed down in a worshipful attitude. Surprised at these actions, Cortez wondered why the Aztecs acted in such a manner. When taken to the Palace, Cortez and his men saw all the gold in the Palace and decided to steal it and take it back to Spain. Montezuma looked at Cortez and wondered if this truly was the great white god? His question was soon answered.

History tells of tremendous battles between the Aztecs and the Conquistadors. This was the time of the Spanish Inquisition and both sides were skilled in methods of torture. During the heat of the battle, both sides took prisoners. But Cortez did not realize what was about to happen to his men captured by the Aztecs. Forcing the prisoners up to their temple, the Aztecs made them climb the stairway in a movement similar to the motions of a serpent or dragon. Upon reaching the top, the victim was stretched out on an altar and held firmly by several men. A drum continued to beat as the natives shouted their mystic chants. Then the priest took his ceremonial knife and cut out the heart of the victim.

Throughout the art of Central America there is evidence of human sacrifice. The cultures of Central America worshiped the same winged serpent god found throughout the world. This god demanded human sacrifice! At one time there was a tremendous civilization in Central America. There are many ruins in this part of the world. The temples with their art tell a story that is to be found all over the world. Atop a number of these temples one can see a reclining stone figure called the CHAC MOOL. He was considered to be the life giver to the various cultures in Central America. On either side of the CHAC MOOL were usually two winged serpents. The mouths are open at the base, the body is the post and the tail is the lintel.

The winged serpent has many forms in the art of Central America. At times it was shown with a man's head or even a man's face inside the mouth of a serpent. Could this represent a demonic power speaking through the serpent with wings? The winged serpent god is frightening when one studies the art and legends of Central America. We can see in pictures the serpent with feathers ready to receive the heart from a human sacrifice. All through the history of this world, there have been human sacrifices in occultism and pagan rituals. It is no wonder that Satan is called the destroyer in the Bible.

Outside Mexico City there are the ruins of a Toltec city called Teotihuacan. According to mythology, this city is the place where the gods came together to create the sun. Teotihuacan was the seat of one of the most advanced cultures of Central America. A Temple can be seen in this ancient ruin that is dedicated to the winged serpent god. The pyramid takes its name from representations of the Mesoamerican "feathered serpent" deity which covered its sides. These are some of the earliest-known representations of the feathered serpent, often identified with the much-later Aztec god Quetzalcoatl.[17] The structure is also known as the **Temple of Quetzalcoatl**, and the **Feathered Serpent Pyramid**.

---

[17] Miller, Mary Ellen; Karl Taube (1993). *The Gods and Symbols of Ancient Mexico and the Maya.* London: Thames and Hudson.

**Figure 4 Chac Mool**

The symbol of the serpent is significant as it represents intellect. The Egyptians often depicted a serpent in the sky as a man riding on its back to the stars. Its role was that of the "separator" or "obstructer." Quetzalcoatl had come to offer them knowledge, wisdom, and understanding of the stars! In return, Quetzalcoatl demanded their souls in the form of human sacrifice as payment for this "knowledge."[18]

Dragon heads are situated throughout the temple. In Figure 5, you can see the serpent descending down the pyramid visible only on the spring and autumn equinoxes. At the rising and setting of the sun, the corner of the structure casts a shadow in the shape of a plumed serpent - Kukulcan, or Quetzalcoatl - along the west side of the north staircase. On these two annual occasions, the shadows from the corner tiers slither down the northern side of the pyramid with the sun's movement to the serpent's head at the base. On the days of the fall and spring equinox,

---

[18] Spencer, Peter, *The Davinci Cult*, 2006, BookSurge, p. 240.

Teotihuacan is packed with folks who dress in white and climb to the top of the Pyramid of the Sun. They stand at the top with arms outstretched to receive the special energy of the site on that day. Once again the Dragon and Winged Serpent are associated together!

It is interesting that all over the world today, in our time, many pagan and witchcraft groups are showing great interest in these old ruins. They are visiting them and seeking to learn their rituals, even holding ceremonies at them! Even the American Indian culture has a winged serpent in their religion. They call it the Phoenix. They think there is some great power to be obtained by finding out what these ancient peoples knew. They did not stop to think that if there were such great power in these horrible places of human sacrifice, why is it that these people, their culture, and their practice of human sacrifice have all been wiped out today? It may be that God allowed this wicked culture to be destroyed because of their cruel and bloodthirsty ways. Satan's religion always brings misery and death-not real power.

Thailand houses a bronze Buddha. Buddha was considered to be the "Enlightened One." His aim was to liberate all things from the endless cycles of birth, death and rebirth that the pagan religions believed in. Buddhism has a powerful influence in the Far East and all over the world. This bronze Buddha has two winged serpents, one on each side. By many, Buddha was considered to be the Life Giver in the Orient. It cannot be a mere accident that in Egypt the Pharaoh, considered to be the Life Giver, had winged serpents on either side of his throne. In Central America, the Chac Mool, the Life Giver, had a winged serpent on each side and in the Orient we find the same thing! The winged serpents on the bronze Buddha in Bangkok are positioned with their heads at the base, the tales come together over the head, and the wings are in the form of a crescent moon at the shoulder.

What is the answer to the mystery of the Dragon and the Winged Serpent? The Bible gives the answer in Revelation 12.

### Revelation 12:7-9 (KJV)
7 And there was war in heaven: Michael and his angels fought against the dragon; and the dragon fought and his angels,
8 And prevailed not; neither was their place found any more in

heaven.

9 And **the great dragon** was cast out, that old serpent, **called the Devil, and Satan, which deceiveth the whole world**: he was cast out into the earth, and his angels were cast out with him.

Here we find the symbols for the devil, being a Dragon and a Serpent. When the devil is pictured as a serpent, he is sly and sneaky. When he is called a Dragon, he is the persecutor. In the last days during the Tribulation, Satan will certainly become the Dragon. Any religion or belief that uses these representations has its roots in pagan Satan worship.

**Figure 5 Pyramid of the Sun AKA Feathered Serpent Pyramid**

The Pyramid of the Sun is one of ancient Mexico's largest structures. It is nearly 200 feet high and 700 feet wide. It is the 3rd largest pyramid in the world. Notice the feathered serpent descending down the temple.

*Chapter 4*

# Giants of Old; Men of Renown

I n order to understand the UFO phenomena, you need to understand that there were "gods" on this earth before the flood of Noah's day and they will appear on this earth again before the 2nd Advent of Jesus Christ. The names of these gods have survived in mythical form in Greek, Roman and Babylonian mythology. The "gods" are those fallen angels whose offspring were the giants.

There are three categories of alien creatures:

1. Humanoid- Grays, Nordics, or the Men in Black

2. Non-humanoid- Reptilian in appearance

3. Hybrids- aliens crossbred with humans

> The purpose of the Reptilians is to deceive humans to revert them to our pre-Edenic state without God.

Let's examine the Reptilians briefly as they tie in with the winged serpents of chapter 3. These reptilian aliens are connected with the UFO phenomena as an occultic legend of a serpent race that seeded mankind, imparted forbidden knowledge, and then watched the development of our evolution. There are widespread ancient legends of these serpent gods who were feared and worshipped from China to Central America.[19] We will look at this in more detail in our discussion of the Mayans. The

---

[19] Written on Mesopotamia day tablets, a Sumerian god called An, was the leader of the Anunaki. One of An's sons, Enki, was the serpent of Eden & who also genetically altered the human race by hybrid beings.

purpose of the Reptilians is to deceive humans to revert them to our pre-Edenic state without God.

Every reference in the Bible concerning those who are "coming" from the heavens is negative and that is why more and more people are not going to tolerate a Bible believer who judges the UFO phenomena and the evolution connection by the Bible.

There are a couple of mysteries concerning the UFOs that we have not yet found the answer for in the Bible. The occupants are not fallen Angels. First of all, they are the wrong size and they come from the wrong source. There are no small or short angels in the Bible. Second, Angels, in the Bible, are males without wings. Third, they are a different race coming from cohabitation between Angels and animals. Fourth, they are always connected with flying machines and no Angel needs a flying machine.

Here is what we know from the Bible. Deception plays a key role! "Take heed that no man deceive you." (Matthew 24:4) "But as the days of Noah were, so shall also the coming of the Son of man be." (Matthew 24:37) So the question is how were the days of Noah? What made those days unique?

### GENESIS 6: 1-2 (KJV)
1 And it came to pass, when men began to multiply on the face of the earth, and daughters were born unto them,
2 That the **sons of God** saw the daughters of men that they were fair; and they took them wives of all which they chose.

They were the men of old, men of renown as the Bible describes them. The Bible clearly uses the "sons of God." The Hebrew word which is used is "Bene Ha Elohim." This always refers to "angels" in the Old Testament.[20] They were not the "Daughters of Men" which is the term "benoth adam" in Hebrew and translates as the "daughters of Adam." It is important to note that "benoth adam" means from Adam; not Cain! Since the designation "sons of God" is consistently used in the Old

---

[20] CF: Job 1:6, 2:1, 38:7 & NT: Luke 20:36

Testament for angels, it is logical to conclude that the term in Genesis 6:2 also referred to angels.

In Job1:6 and Job 2:1 the "sons of God" came to present themselves before the Lord in heaven. Among them is Satan-a further confirmation that the "sons of God" are angels.

### Job 1:6 (KJV)
⁶ Now there was a day when the sons of God came to present themselves before the LORD, and Satan came also among them.

Job 38:7 says the "sons of God" shouted for joy when God laid the foundations of the earth. Angels are the only entities that fit this designation since man has not been created at that time!

## THE NEPHILIM

### Genesis 6:4 (KJV)
4 There were **giants** in the earth in those days; and also after that, when the sons of God came in unto the daughters of men, and they bare *children* to them, the same *became* mighty men which *were* of old, men of renown.

The word the Hebrew uses here is the word "Nephilim" which means "the fallen ones" and HaGibborim which means "the mighty ones." The Greek Septuagint (LXX), a translation of the Torah into Greek about 270 B.C., renders these as gigantes; meaning "earth-born." These giants are the result of an unnatural union between some of the fallen angels and human women that resulted in offspring that were not only gigantic in stature but very evil. Their great size and strength likely came from the mixture of demonic "DNA" mixing with human genetics. Does that make them ancient aliens from other planets as some suppose? No. They are not extraterrestrials at all! They are hyper-dimensional in nature. After the Nephilim arrive, we see that wickedness abounds on the earth corrupting mankind. This was one of the primary reasons for the drastic judgment of the flood.

**Genesis 6:5-9 (KJV)**

[5] And GOD saw that the wickedness of man *was* great in the earth, and *that* every imagination of the thoughts of his heart *was* only evil continually.

[6] And it repented the LORD that he had made man on the earth, and it grieved him at his heart.

[7] And the LORD said, I will destroy man whom I have created from the face of the earth; both man, and beast, and the creeping thing, and the fowls of the air; for it repenteth me that I have made them.

[8] But Noah found grace in the eyes of the LORD.

[9] These *are* the generations of Noah: Noah was a just man *and* **perfect in his generations**, *and* Noah walked with God.

This intermarrying with the Fallen Angels is the reason that God wipes out everyone except for Noah and his family in a worldwide flood. Every human genetic line had been corrupted except for Noah's. It wasn't because Noah was a perfect man! The Bible doesn't say that. It says that he was "perfect in his generations." Noah and his family were not corrupted by the Nephilim and were the only ones to carry on the human gene pool to repopulate the earth after the Deluge. They were "perfect" in their DNA. This corruption of the human genetics with the Fallen Angels is Satan's attempt to pollute the human gene pool to attempt to thwart the coming birth of the Messiah!

So the Nephilim were the offspring of the cohabitation of fallen angels with human women. What we have in Genesis 6 is part of the Angels that rebelled with Lucifer come down and cohabited with human women; producing a race of demonic giants.

The story of the Nephilim is chronicled more fully in the Book of Enoch[21]. The sons of God (fallen angels) descended first onto Mt. Hermon which means "desolation." The Greek, Aramaic, and main Ge'ez manuscripts of 1 Enoch and Jubilees obtained in the 19th century

---

[21] An ancient Jewish religious book traditionally ascribed to Enoch, the great-grandfather of Noah. It is not part of the biblical canon. It was also discovered among the Dead Sea Scrolls.

and held in the British Museum and Vatican Library, connect the origin of the Nephilim with the fallen angels, and in particular with the "Watchers."[22]   Samyaza, an angel of high rank, is described in the Book of Enoch as leading a rebel sect of angels in a descent to earth to have sexual intercourse with human females:

> "And it came to pass when the children of men had multiplied that in those days were born unto them beautiful and comely daughters. And the angels, the children of the heaven, saw and lusted after them, and said to one another: 'Come, let us choose us wives from among the children of men and beget us children.' And Semjaza, who was their leader, said unto them: 'I fear ye will not indeed agree to do this deed, and I alone shall have to pay the penalty of a great sin.' And they all answered him and said: 'Let us all swear an oath, and all bind ourselves by mutual imprecations not to abandon this plan but to do this thing.' Then sware they all together and bound themselves by mutual imprecations upon it. And they were in all two hundred; who descended in the days of Jared on the summit of Mount Hermon, and they called it Mount Hermon, because they had sworn and bound themselves by mutual imprecations upon it..."[23]

In addition to Enoch, the Book of Jubilees[24] (7:21–25) also states that ridding the Earth of these Nephilim was one of God's purposes for flooding the Earth in Noah's time. An Old Testament patriarch, Jared or Yeh-red, was named because in his days the angels descended upon the earth.   Yaw-rad means to "descend." This ancient book describes the Nephilim as being evil giants.

Admittedly, this is pretty wild. Now that the human race is starting, Satan sees an opportunity to do that which he could not do before and that is to be fruitful and multiply. How does he do this? He does so by getting some of the fallen Angels (sons of God) that rebuild

---

[22] The Watchers is a term found in the Book of Enoch referring to the fallen angels.

[23] http://www.ancienttexts.org/library/ethiopian/enoch/1watchers/watchers.htm

[24] Sometimes called **Lesser Genesis** (**Leptogenesis**) is an ancient Jewish religious book well known to Early Christianity.

with him to cohabit with the daughters of men. This produces a race of demigods; half demonic, half human giants.

It must be pointed out here that all the fallen angels were not used in this way. Those that did cohabit lost their spiritual estate and the Psalms say they died in the flood like men. After their physical bodies died, they were chained under darkness waiting the Day of Judgment. However, not every angel that rebelled with Satan is chained in hell. We know they are still free to fight with the archangel Michael and the angels in heaven in the middle of the Tribulation of the last days. So these are the angels that sinned. They are also described in Jude 6-7.

### Jude 1:6 (KJV)
[6] And the angels which kept not their first estate, but left their own habitation, he hath reserved in everlasting chains under darkness unto the judgment of the great day.

### 2 Peter 2:4-5 (KJV)
[4] For if God spared not the angels that sinned, but cast *them* down to hell, and delivered *them* into chains of darkness, to be reserved unto judgment;
[5] And spared not the old world, but saved Noah the eighth *person*, a preacher of righteousness, bringing in the flood upon the world of the ungodly;

Before we go any further, let's address some objections to what we are reading. Does the Bible ever talk about any of the angels that were in heaven rebelling with Lucifer? The answer is "yes." If you recall Revelation 12 we saw that 1/3 of the angels followed Lucifer.

### Revelation 12:3 (KJV)
[3] And there appeared another wonder in heaven; and behold a great red dragon, having seven heads and ten horns, and seven crowns upon his heads.

Now we need to identify the Dragon.

### Revelation 12:9 (KJV)

[9] And the great dragon was cast out, that old serpent, called the Devil, and Satan, which deceiveth the whole world: he was cast out into the earth, and his angels were cast out with him.

Now, we go back to where we left off to see the action that the Dragon is taking.

### Revelation 12:4 (KJV)

4 And his tail drew the third part of the **stars of heaven**, and did cast them to the earth:

So the Dragon drew the third part of the stars which now helps us to identify the "stars". Let's pick it up in verse 12.

### Revelation 1:12-16 (KJV)

[12] And I turned to see the voice that spake with me. And being turned, I saw seven golden candlesticks;
[13] And in the midst of the seven candlesticks *one* like unto the Son of man, clothed with a garment down to the foot, and girt about the paps with a golden girdle.
[14] His head and *his* hairs *were* white like wool, as white as snow; and his eyes *were* as a flame of fire;
[15] And his feet like unto fine brass, as if they burned in a furnace; and his voice as the sound of many waters.
[16] And he had in his right hand **seven stars**: and out of his mouth went a sharp twoedged sword: and his countenance *was* as the sun shineth in his strength.

Now we see the "stars" are identified for John as Angels in verse 20.

### Revelation 1:20 (KJV)

[20] The mystery of the seven stars which thou sawest in my right hand, and the seven golden candlesticks. **The seven stars are the angels** of the seven churches: and the seven candlesticks which thou sawest are the seven churches.

Also, we see an angel described as a star in Revelation 9.

### Revelation 9:1-2 (KJV)

[1] And the fifth angel sounded, and I saw a <u>star</u> fall from heaven unto the earth: and <u>*to him*</u> was given the key of the bottomless pit.
[2] And he opened the bottomless pit; and there arose a smoke out of the pit, as the smoke of a great furnace; and the sun and the air were darkened by reason of the smoke of the pit.

Also we see that there was war in heaven where the devil and his angels fight against Michael and his angels. The result was that the devil (the Dragon) and his angels were cast out of heaven.

### Revelation 12:6-9 (KJV)

[6] And the woman fled into the wilderness, where she hath a place prepared of God, that they should feed her there a thousand two hundred *and* threescore days.
[7] And there was war in heaven: Michael and his angels fought against the dragon; and the dragon fought and <u>*his angels*</u>,
[8] And prevailed not; neither was their place found any more in heaven.
[9] And the great dragon was cast out, that old serpent, called the Devil, and Satan, which deceiveth the whole world: he was cast out into the earth, and <u>*his angels were cast out*</u> with him.

> The spiritual beings referred to as "sons of God" in the Old Testament are Angels.

## SONS OF GOD

Next, let's address who the "sons of God" are in Genesis 6:4. They are called that because they are created as spiritual beings; *in the image of God* (God is a spirit). As spirits, they are part of the Kingdom of God, which is the spiritual kingdom. A man can't get into that kingdom until he is born again spiritually since he is born into this world in the physical realm; but spiritually dead because of sin. Only after a man is born again can a person become a "son of God" in the spiritual rebirth.

The spiritual beings referred to as "sons of God" in the Old Testament are Angels. The next thing you should know is that every reference to angels in the Bible is male. That is, there are no female angels anywhere in Scripture. I know this runs against the common pictures that grace the Christian bookstores, that if you are going to study the Bible it is best not to get your doctrine from artwork. Paintings depicting female angels and angels with wings are not Biblical. Additionally, angels described in the Bible never have wings. Angels are not sexless, but always appear in scripture as wingless males. The men of Sodom thought the angels were men and wanted to have sex with them. So did Abraham when he entertained them prior to their entering Sodom. And the New Testament tells us "some have entertained angels unaware." Wings however, are associated with Cherubim and Seraphim's; as well as female demons.[25] Notice that Cherubim and Seraphim have wings, but neither have only two, they have 4 to 6 wings each! The sons of God that married the daughters of men were fallen angels. Furthermore, when fallen angels produced children from human women, the offspring were giants.

Sons of God are defined in Job chapters 1, 2, & 38. They are present before Adam is created (Job 38:7). They are also the "gods" of Psalm 82:1 and Psalm 89:6. (Note the flood in the context.) These sons of God may have been around before Noah up to 800 years before his time.

The next thing to address is the "sons of God" and the "daughters of men" reference, the objection being that Angels are sexless. But the bible says angels can't have sex doesn't it? No it doesn't. Matthew 22:30 answers this question whether angels can reproduce. It says they don't *marry*. Notice "in heaven" is the qualifier. The idea comes from a note in the Scofield reference Bible, which I have a great deal of respect for. But the notes do not overrule the Bible.

---

[25] CF: Zechariah 5:4-11

# LINE OF SETH THEORY

One school of thought that circulates these days, in order to prevent folk from believing what they read in the Bible, is to say that the "sons of God" represent the godly line of Seth, while the "daughters of men" represent the ungodly line of Cain. This view will keep you from having to believe that the Bible has anything outlandish in it or that it is a very civilized book that must conform to our ideas. Look, it's a free country and everyone in a democracy is entitled to his or her opinion about things, but we are talking about a book with absolute truth in it. We are talking about the inspired, preserved, infallible word of God. Your idea or mine is worth absolutely nothing; the only thing that matters is what that Book says. And if you are going to study the Bible and get anything out of it you had better get that straight in your mind. God has revealed truth to us, and we had better handle it carefully and properly.

So let's examine this "godly line of Seth" argument. First of all, there is no such thing in the Bible as a "godly line." There is a Messianic line, but it is a far cry from a "godly line," since it contains adulterers, murderers, harlots, liars and the like. If that qualifies to be a "godly line," then there has never been an ungodly line of any kind on the planet. Secondly, the Bible never defines "sons of God" as a godly line. Neither does it define the "line of Seth" as a godly line. Also, as we have already examined, the union of the sons of God and the daughters of men produced a race of giants. There is nothing in the Bible or in human history that leads us to believe that a race of godly people, marrying ungodly people, would produce a race of giants. If that were the case, we would have giants today aplenty. Let's be honest, when godly people marry ungodly people their children are not giants.

Some answer this by saying that the Bible did not mean that they were giants physically, but mentally. Again, we do not have license to read things into the Bible just because we are uncomfortable with what we read. In a moment you will see that these "giants" showed up again in the Promised Land and they were not giants intellectually, they were giants physically. At least that is the testimony of those that saw them. Are we supposed to believe that the eyewitnesses were mistaken or misleading? What they said was that compared to these giants, the normal men of Israel were like grasshoppers. That is a comparison of size, not mental ability. Have you ever heard anyone refer to someone's I.Q. by comparing him to a grasshopper? I didn't think so. Here is the idea for those of you who still don't get it. Giants are BIG, grasshoppers are SMALL. Get it? It's a comparison of physical size. Goliath was one of these giants along with others named in the Bible. They were the product of the intermarrying of fallen sons of God with human women.

For the sake of argument let us suppose for a moment that Genesis 6 is describing a line of 'godly' people intermarrying with a line of 'ungodly' people. Since all of the 'ungodly' line was destroyed in the flood (only 8 of the "godly line" survived) how can we account for the giants showing up again after the flood? The line of Cain (the ungodly line) should have all drowned in the flood. Why, even the passage tells us that they were not only here before Noah's ark, but also after that.

**Genesis 6:4 (KJV)**
4 There were giants in the earth in those days; **and also after that**, when the sons of God came in unto the daughters of men, and they bare children to them, the same became mighty men which were of old, men of renown.

"And also after that" is a reference to AFTER THAT! Do we see any giants on the scene, after that? Yes, we do. When the children of Israel go into the Promised Land, it is a land flowing with milk and honey and GIANTS!

**Numbers 13:33 (KJV)**
33 And there we saw the giants, the sons of Anak, which come of the giants: and we were in our own sight as grasshoppers, and so we were in their sight.

That would be what the "and also after that" is a reference to. And since the alleged 'ungodly' line was drowned in the flood, the question remains, where did they come from 'after that'? The only scriptural support we have is that the Nephilim are back in play just as they were in Genesis 6. No, they didn't survive the flood by hanging on to the ark. Nor did they survive the flood waters. No. Those giants were all destroyed in the Great Deluge. It is simply a replay of the same old trick. Only this time, the play is to now prevent Israel from entering the Promise Land that was granted to Abraham and stop them from becoming the promised nation that will usher in the King and His Kingdom.

The Nephilim had returned!

As we have shown, there never was an ungodly line and a godly line, but rather "sons of God" (Job 1, 2, 38) and "daughters of men." Seth may be in a "Messianic line," but that would be the end of it; there is no "godly line." As explained earlier, Seth was no son of God, for he did not have the image of God restored to him. He was still in the image of his father, Adam.

Here are the races of giants the Bible describes:

1. Rephaim - from the root rapha = spirits, shades; the walking dead. (Gen. 14:5, Deuteronomy 3:11, Isaiah 26:14) Gen 14 is the account of how powerful Chedorlaomer, King of Elam, was by defeating the kings of Sodom, Gomorrah, Rephaims, Zuzims, Emims, Horites, Amalekites and the Amorites. These were the nations of the Giants. We also read how Abram defeated Chedorlaomer in battle to rescue Lot when he invaded Sodom & Gomorrah. This was a sign to let all know that God was with Abram!

A descendant of the Rephaim living at the time of Moses was named King Og.

> **Deuteronomy 3:11 (KJV)**
> [11] For only Og king of Bashan remained of the remnant of giants; behold, his bedstead *was* a bedstead of iron; *is* it not in Rabbath of the children of Ammon? nine cubits *was* the length thereof, and four cubits the breadth of it, after the cubit of a man.

A standard cubit was 18 inches. A royal cubit was 21 inches. Some scholars also say that a royal cubit was the length of the forefinger to the elbow or the length of the first born son. Using these measurements, we can estimate King Og's height at 13 to 15ft tall! He was one of the last remaining remnants of the giants at the time of Moses.

**Joshua 13:12 (KJV)**
[12] All the kingdom of Og in Bashan, which reigned in Ashtaroth and in Edrei, who remained of the remnant of the giants: **for these did Moses smite**, and cast them out.

Did you notice how long the giants were around after the flood? In these two verses that you just read they span from the time of Abraham, to the 400 years of captivity of the Israelites in Egypt, until the time of Moses. But we also see Joshua fighting the Anakims as well.

2. Anakim "Ananaki" – those from who the heavens came (Num. 13:33) They were perhaps the best known of the giants living in the land of Caanan at the time of the Exodus. Let's read the full account so we maintain the context.

**Numbers 13:28-33 (KJV)**
[28] Nevertheless the people *be* strong that dwell in the land, and the cities *are* walled, *and* very great: and moreover we saw the **children of Anak** there.
[29] The Amalekites dwell in the land of the south: and the Hittites, and the Jebusites, and the Amorites, dwell in the mountains: and the Canaanites dwell by the sea, and by the coast of Jordan.
[30] And Caleb stilled the people before Moses, and said, Let us go up at once, and possess it; for we are well able to overcome it.
[31] But the men that went up with him said, We be not able to go up against the people; for they *are* stronger than we.
[32] And they brought up an evil report of the land which they had searched unto the children of Israel, saying, The land, through which we have gone to search it, *is* a land that eateth up the inhabitants thereof; and all the people that we saw in it *are* men of a great stature.
[33] **And there we saw the giants, the sons of Anak**, *which*

*come* of the giants: and we were in our own sight as grasshoppers, and so we were in their sight.

**Joshua 14:15 (KJV)**
<sup>15</sup> And the name of Hebron before *was* Kirjatharba; *which Arba was* a great man among the Anakims. And the land had rest from war.

So the city of Hebron where Abraham, Isaac, and Jacob settled was also called Kirjatharba. Anak is the son of Arba; hence the name "Anakims". But Arba was the greatest among the Anakims. Joshua fights many battles with the Anakim; ultimately destroying most of them.

**Joshua 11:21-22 (KJV)**
<sup>21</sup> And at that time came Joshua, and cut off the Anakims from the mountains, from Hebron, from Debir, from Anab, and from all the mountains of Judah, and from all the mountains of Israel: Joshua destroyed them utterly with their cities.
<sup>22</sup> There was none of the Anakims left in the land of the children of Israel: only in Gaza, in Gath, and in Ashdod, there remained.

Next, the shepherd boy takes on the famous giant from Gath. This is where the remaining Anakims lived. We know the account as the battle of David and Goliath.

**1 Samuel 17:4-7 (KJV)**
<sup>4</sup> And there went out a champion out of the camp of the Philistines, named Goliath, of Gath, whose height *was* six cubits and a span.
<sup>5</sup> And *he had* an helmet of brass upon his head, and he *was* armed with a coat of mail; and the weight of the coat *was* five thousand shekels of brass.
<sup>6</sup> And *he had* greaves of brass upon his legs, and a target of brass between his shoulders.
<sup>7</sup> And the staff of his spear *was* like a weaver's beam; and his spear's head *weighed* six hundred shekels of iron: and one bearing a shield went before him.

Goliath would have been between 9-11 ft. in height using the prior definitions of a cubit. If you continue to read the narrative you should notice an important detail.

> **1 Samuel 17:40 (KJV)**
> [40] And he took his staff in his hand, and chose him five smooth stones out of the brook, and put them in a shepherd's bag which he had, even in a scrip; and his sling *was* in his hand: and he drew near to the Philistine.

Did you see it? Why do you think David picked up five smooth stones? It was because Goliath had four brothers. David was ready for all five!

# 4 MORE BATTLES

In Second Samuel we read of the next four battles that King David and his men had with Goliath's four brothers.

> **2 Samuel 21:15-22 (KJV)**
> [15] Moreover the Philistines had yet war again with Israel; and David went down, and his servants with him, and fought against the Philistines: and David waxed faint.
> [16] And **Ishbibenob**, which *was* of the sons of the giant, the weight of whose spear *weighed* three hundred *shekels* of brass in weight, he being girded with a new *sword*, thought to have slain David.
> [17] But Abishai the son of Zeruiah succoured him, and smote the Philistine, and killed him. Then the men of David sware unto him, saying, Thou shalt go no more out with us to battle, that thou quench not the light of Israel.
> [18] And it came to pass after this, that there was again a battle with the Philistines at Gob: then Sibbechai the Hushathite slew **Saph**, which *was* of the sons of the giant.
> [19] And there was again a battle in Gob with the Philistines, where Elhanan the son of Jaareoregim, a Bethlehemite, slew *the brother of* Goliath the Gittite, the staff of whose spear *was*

like a weaver's beam.

²⁰ And there was yet a battle in Gath, where was a man of *great* stature, that had **on every hand six fingers**, and on **every foot six toes**, four and twenty in number; and he also was born to the giant.

²¹ And when he defied Israel, Jonathan the son of Shimea the brother of David slew him.

²² These four were born to the giant in Gath, and fell by the hand of David, and by the hand of his servants.

Now in verse 19 a name is not given. But it is given in First Chronicles 20:5. Let's read the parallel account.

**1 Chronicles 20:4-8 (KJV)**

⁴ And it came to pass after this, that there arose war at Gezer with the Philistines; at which time Sibbechai the Hushathite slew Sippai, *that was* of the children of the giant: and they were subdued.

⁵ And there was war again with the Philistines; and Elhanan the son of Jair slew **Lahmi the brother of Goliath the Gittite**, whose spear staff *was* like a weaver's beam.

⁶ And yet again there was war at Gath, where was a man of *great* stature, whose fingers and toes *were* four and twenty, six *on each hand*, and six *on each foot*: and he also was the son of the giant.

⁷ But when he defied Israel, Jonathan the son of Shimea David's brother slew him.

⁸ These were born unto the giant in Gath; and they fell by the hand of David, and by the hand of his servants.

So now we have three of the four names of these giants- Ishbibenob, Sippai (Saph), and Lahmi. The fourth is not named. We only read the description of his hands and feet.

3. Emim - the proud deserters; terrors.

**Deuteronomy 2:10-11 (KJV)**
¹⁰ The Emims dwelt therein in times past, a people great, and

many, and tall, as the Anakims;
[11] Which also were accounted giants, as the Anakims; but the Moabites call them Emims.

4. Zuzim - the evil ones, roaming things (Gen. 14:5)

5. Zamzummims - the evil plotters, (Genesis 19:38; Deut. 2:20-21) They were a people great, and tall, as the Anakims and were overcome by the Ammonites, who called them "Zamzummims." They belonged to the Rephaim, and inhabited the country afterwards occupied by the Ammonites. It is thought that they might be Ham-zuzims (Zuzims) dwelling in Ham; a place to the south of Ashteroth (Gen_14:5), the ancient Rabbath-ammon.

## GIANT REMAINS IN ANCIENT HISTORY [26]

✓ Remains of Teutobochus in Rhone in 1613; 30' tall.

✓ Angoula; 21' tall or 12 cubits in height.

✓ Giants of Patagonia; 11-15' tall

✓ Giant skulls in Siberia- 2009 (Omsk Museum of History in Russia)

✓ Giant skulls in Bolivia near the Gateway of the Sun- 8', 6" skeletons

✓ Ashland County, Ohio 1879- 9',8" skeleton

✓ Giants of Lovelock, Nevada in 1911- 6', 6"

✓ Giant Indian skeleton at Panther Cave; Glen Rose, Texas 1947- 7' tall

---

[26] Taylor, Joe, Giants Against Evolution, Mt. Blanco Publishing, 2012

# Maximinus Thrax

Imperator Caesar Gaius
Iulius Verus Maximinus Pius
Felix Invictus Augustus
Augustus
235–238

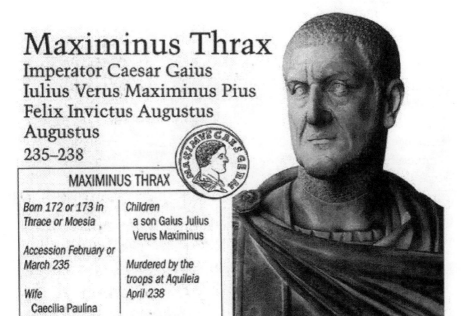

| MAXIMINUS THRAX | |
|---|---|
| Born 172 or 173 in Thrace or Moesia | Children<br>  a son Gaius Julius<br>  Verus Maximinus |
| Accession February or March 235 | Murdered by the troops at Aquileia April 238 |
| Wife<br>  Caecilia Paulina | |

Maximinus was probably the biggest man ever to hold the office of Roman emperor. The Historia Augusta has it that he was 8 ft 6 in (2.6 m) tall, and so strong that he could pull laden carts unaided! The size of his footwear was also legendary, and the expression 'Maximinus's boot' came to be used in popular parlance for any tall or lanky individual. Surviving portrait busts, such as this one from the Louvre, show Maximinus as a heavily-muscled man with powerful jaw and close-cropped hair, the image of a seasoned soldier. Not for him the meditative, spiritual pose favoured by Alexander Severus.

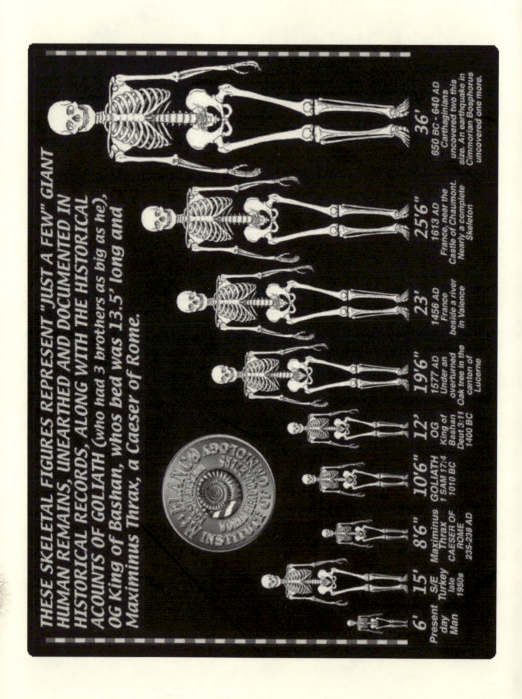

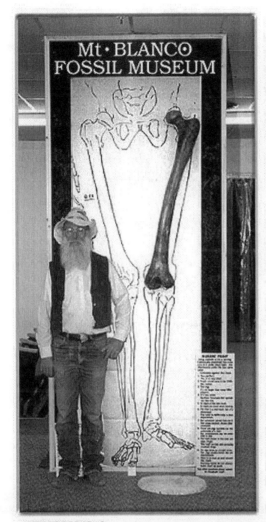

## 47 inch Human Femur

In the late 1950s, during road construction in south-east Turkey in the Euphrates Valley, many tombs containing the remains of Giants were uncovered.
At two sites the leg bones were measured to be about 120 cms "47.24 inches".
Joe Taylor, Director of the Mt. BLANCO FOSSIL MUSEUM in Crosbyton, Texas, was commissioned to sculpt this anatomically correct, and to scale, human femur.
This "Giant" stood some 14-16 feet tall, and had 20-22 inch long feet. His or Her finger tips, with arms to their sides, would be about 6 feet above the ground.
The Biblical record, in Deuteronomy 3:11 states that the Iron Bed of Og, King of Bashan was 9 cubits by 4 cubits or approximately 14 feet long by 6 feet wide!

**GENESIS 6:4** —
*There were Nephilim (Giants) in the earth in those days; and also after that when the sons of God (Angels?) came in unto the daughters of men, and they bare children to them, the same became mighty men which were of old, men of renown.*

More Info & Replicas available at mtblanco1@aol.com or www.mtblanco.com
Mt. Blanco Fossil Museum • P.O. Box 559, Crosbyton, TX 79322 • 1-800-367-7454

**Giant fossil footprint, Glen Rose, TX. - Author A.S. Judkins next to a 24" track that was excavated in the early 1980's along the Paluxy River.**

**Figure 6 Winged creature from the Palace of King Sargon of Assyria (Isaiah 20)**

*Chapter 5*

# Mystery of the Sphinx

At the midpoint of the Tribulation, Satan and his rebel angels are "cast down to the earth, a place no longer found for them in heaven." At that time, the devil and his powers of the air will be forced to remain on the earth to be judged by almighty God.

While Satan is still able to navigate the heavenly regions, and even "walk to and fro *in* the earth" (Job), he is setting up the world to accept the fallen angels as "aliens" or inter-dimensional beings of some sort.

If Satan's goals could be summed up and prioritized, they would appear this way:

1. Stop the redemption of man by preventing the atonement of Jesus on the cross.

2. Since #1 failed, prevent human kind from ever hearing or understanding the gospel.

3. Prevent at all cost, the resurrection of the dead.

4. Since the gathering together of all the rebel angels and their imprisonment on earth for judgment is declared by God, great preparations must be made to utilize this event for the continuation of deception.

5. Prevent the eventual reign of God in human form on the earth.

The key to understanding the celestial zodiac, surprisingly, is found in the enigmatic figure of the ancient sphinx.

Satan knows his future and his fallen angels must prepare the world for their impending arrival. The main focus of their preparation is to create an open and welcome environment for their imminent return in the future as the "gods."

Satan has taken all the major references, all topology, and prophecy regarding the first and second comings of Jesus Christ and twisted the information to fit the end time "working of error." There is a body of non-biblical prophecy that has been disseminated throughout the world via folklore, myth, media, and popular culture. Myths can be viewed as foreshadowing the facts of Scripture, or as corruptions of them. This view, which is not contemporarily popular, is surprisingly enlightening when attention is focused on meaning of names, characters and places of Classical myth in relation to Biblical stories.

The most relevant and necessary tool for discernment of theological interpretation of myth is a foundation of understanding concerning the origins and meaning of the celestial zodiac.

### Psalm 19:1 (KJV)
1 The heavens declare the glory of God; and the firmament sheweth his handywork.

Most Christians recoil at the thought of delving into the profane practice of Astrology even if merely studying it from a comparative distance. The Bible is clear about God's condemnation of the practice of Astrology. However, one needs to keep in mind the modus operandi of the Enemy. Satan focuses his lies and distortions in the most effective places. These places are without exception, where God's truth is revealed. Since the most effective and believable lie is one sandwiched between two truths, so it is with the Zodiac.

**Figure 7 Assyrian-winged Sphinx from the 9th century B.C.**

**Figure 8 King Hiram of Byblos on a Phoenician Cherubim throne. This bas relief is from his sarcophagus. These Cherubhim have been identified as Winged Sphinxes Moscati dates the sarchopagus to the 13th-12th century B.C. that is about 300 years before King Solomon.[27]**

The pictures found today in the zodiac were not developed by the Greeks, but were in place perhaps as early as 4000 B.C. predating even the civilizations of Sumeria. These pictures were not merely arranged in haphazard order to aid in the tracking of the star movements, but with the purpose of depicting an epic narrative.

This understanding of the zodiac reveals an intelligence and prophetic understanding that was corrupted through time by "the opposer." The zodiac was never intended to be monitored to reveal destiny, with the stars in control of men's lives. Rather it was established as a pictorial story of God's plan of salvation on earth. God is in control

---

[27] Sabatino Moscati. The Phoenicians. Gruppo Editoriale Fabbri Bompiani, Sonzono, p. 127. Etas S.p.A. Milan. March 1988.

of the stars and men. The key to understanding the celestial zodiac, surprisingly, is found in the enigmatic figure of the ancient sphinx.

Sphinxes were usually placed at entrances to palaces or temples of antiquity. This positioning implied power, authority and protection. The bodily form the sphinx is always a combination of at least two of four animals, a lion, bull or eagle with the head of a human. The combination of all four creatures in one constitutes what is called in Hebrew, a "kerubim" or cherub. The word kerubim means "one who prays" or "one who intercedes". The Bible also defines cherubim as a type or order of angel. Sphinx is an aggregate of at least two of four creatures, always the same four, which represent what the Bible calls cherubim, a type of angel.

**Fallen Angels kneeling beside the Tree of Life- Palace of Nimrod**

Why were angels depicted in antiquity as sphinx? What is the meaning behind the four earthly creatures that compose them? Contrary to modern astrology, the true meaning of the celestial zodiac and the symbols of the ecliptic, the course the sun appears to travel the heavens, have been lost to the majority of mankind. However, its purpose can be understood if one connects the sequence of pictures in story form.

In Egyptian hieroglyphs the sphinx was called Neb meaning "the lord." Sphinx in Greek means to "connect or bind together". A sphinx combines the head of a woman and the body of a lion. This fixes the benchmark for the beginning and ending of the celestial narrative; beginning with Virgo and ending with Leo.

Dr. Robert Schoch, Geologist, who has studied the Sphinx extensively, has concluded that it was created between 7000-5000 B.C.[28] In other words, between 5,000-10,000 years ago! This is contrary to the traditional date of 2500 B.C. Fossil remains in the limestone of both the temple and the sphinx are the same, suggesting that they were built during the same time period *predating* Khufu. However, Schoch's conclusions are not accepted by traditional Egyptologists. Most scholars think the Sphinx is post-Flood.

## THE MAZZAROTH

The twelve major constellations, along with their decans (minor constellations), present the story of the ages in the form of a play. Act One is presented through the first four constellations — Virgo, Libra, Scorpio, and Sagittarius. It begins in Bethlehem with the birth of the *"Seed"* of the woman, and establishes his conflict with and victory over Scorpio — the *"seed"* of the serpent. Act Two is presented through four constellations — Capricorn, Aquarius, Pisces and Aries. They represent the Church Age and New Testament Christianity, whose astronomical symbol is a fish. The last four constellations, along with their decans, represent the concluding act in the great drama of the ages — The Tribulation Period followed by the Second Coming of Christ. It is presented through the constellations Taurus, Gemini, Cancer, and Leo.

Between 2000 B.C. and 1 A.D., the sun rose into the constellation Aries; the lamb prepared from the foundations of the world, the unblemished sacrifice for mankind with his foot poised to strike off the tether attaching the fishes to the neck of the sea monster. "He (Jesus Christ) came to set the captives free." Today our sun rises in the constellation Pisces; the fishes connected to the neck of the sea monster, one points to the center of heaven the other follows the ecliptic, the path of the earth around the sun. "Thy kingdom come, thy will be done on earth

---

[28] Robert Schoch, "Regarding the Great Sphinx of Giza," *KMT: A Modern Journal of Ancient Egypt*, vol. 3 no. 2, 1992

as it is in heaven." In the future, it will rise in the constellation Aquarius; the water bearer, the one pouring out life-giving waters that symbolize God's spirit, into the mouth of the fish. The beta star in the other shoulder=who goeth and returneth!

The sign of Taurus will be Act Three, showing us the coming of the Judge of all the earth. Taurus is pictured as a raging bull, who is coming furiously. His horns, symbolizing God's judgment, are pointed to the earth, one stabs the heel of a shepherd "Aquilla", who holds his flock, Christ the good shepherd, received in our place God's absolute judgment. Only the front half of the bull is depicted in the constellation. Where the back end of the bull would normally be drawn stands the constellation Aries, the Lamb — as if the bull is coming out of Aires. It is a magnificent picture of Christ who came the first time as the Lamb of God to take away the sins of the world, but will return one day bringing judgment upon the wicked. In the bull's neck is Pleiades, the congregating of the judges, who come back to earth after their resurrection to judge the earth with Christ at his second coming.

A decan to Taurus is Orion, which is one of the most spectacular and wonderful sights in the night sky. Orion is pictured as a mighty hunter with a club in his right hand. In his left hand, he holds the skin of a lion that he has killed. Orion is mentioned twice in the book of Job and once in the prophecy of Amos. Orion means "coming forth as light." The brightest star in the constellation is *Betelgeuse*, meaning "the coming of the branch." Another star in his foot is *Rigel*, meaning "the foot that crushes." In the shoulder of the constellation is a star called *Bellatrix*, meaning "quickly coming." In his leg is a star called *Saiph* meaning, "bruised." Again, as in every other case, we are reminded of Christ crushing the head of the serpent. Orion is obviously a picture of Christ coming in power and great glory.

What about the four creatures of a cherub? Look at the four brightest stars in the zodiac.

1. Fomalhaut, in Aquarius (man)

2. Regulus, in Leo (lion)

3. Antares, in Opheocus, (serpent holder or eagle)

4. Aldebaran in Taurus, (the bull).

The Zodiac or the "Mazzaroth" as the Bible calls it has laid out the signs to also match the four beasts beginning with the virgin (Virgo) and ending with the sign of the lion (Leo-the lion of the tribe of Judah)! They are also laid out so that the sign of the man (Aquarius the water carrier), the sign of the lion (Leo), the sign of the ox or bull, (Taurus) and the eagle (Serpent Holder) are at the four points of the constellations! All four of these stars are arranged three signs apart, in the four corners of the heavens. These are the four creatures which combine to form the scriptural cherubim!

When the zodiac was arranged these stars appeared on the horizon corresponding to the spring and fall equinoxes and the summer and winter solstices.[29] These four stars rose before the sun in the east in sequence with the four seasons. Since the precession of the equinoxes completes its cycle in 14,000 years, the earth's position relative to these stars has changed and they no longer mark the seasons. The constellations rarely if ever imply the shapes found in the zodiac, yet the sequence and the types have remained consistent from greatest antiquity to this day. The answer to the mystery behind the zodiac and its apparent narrative can be found in the ancient symbols themselves, their relation to each other and their correspondence to prophecy in the Bible.[30]

David knew the meanings of the names of the stars. The names of the stars were terms commonly used in the Messianic prophecies and aspirations of God's ancient people. David could point to the brightest stars in the sky and ponder on their significance.

Spica= The Branch

Arcturus= He Comes

---

[29] Biblical Archaeology Review, vol. 20,#5 pp. 40-53
[30] Kennedy, James, *The Real Meaning of the Zodiac*, CRM Publishing, 1997

Pollux=Who Comes to Suffer

Antaries= The Wounded

Sirius= The Prince

Elnath= The Slain

Procyon= The Redeemer

Vega= He shall be Exalted

> This is the whole story of God's atonement work on earth; its beginning and ending are symbolized by the Sphinx!

**Virgo** is depicted as a virgin in every ancient reference, holding in one hand a branch, and in on the other a sheaf or grain, or seed, always associated with a child, "Shesh nu" in Egyptian, the desired son, the symbol of the incarnation of God on earth.

**Libra**, the scales or in the earliest zodiacs, an altar. Its meaning is the measuring of a price. One of its stars in Arabic means, "the price which is deficient," while opposite is a star whose name means, "the price which covers," or atonement. Libra symbolizes the price of the conflict, the deficient works of man compared to the perfect and finished sacrifice of Jesus accomplished on the cross.

**Scorpio**, with his claws reaching out to influence the scales, is crushed beneath the foot of Opheucus, the serpent holder, who in earliest times was depicted as an eagle. Opheucus's foot is stung by the upraised tail of the scorpion, his other foot is above the scorpion's heart. He restrains the serpent coiled around him from taking the crown. Opheucus depicts the earliest prophecy in the Bible, "I will put enmity between the serpent and the offspring of the women, it will strike at his heel, and he will crush (the serpent's) head."

**Sagittarius**, in the oldest pictures of the zodiac **is a cherubim**. This symbol is situated 1/3rd of the way around the zodiacal circle. It had the body of both lion and bull with wings of an eagle and the head of a man. **Sagittarius is the symbol of the incarnation, both God and man**, animals representing the four corners of the heavens and symbolizing the aspects of God's redemptive work on this earth, he is poised with his arrow drawn and pointed at the heart of the scorpion. Underneath him is the Southern Cross.

**Capricorn**, the goat with the tail of the fish. To the Hebrews, **the goat was the sin offering,** Capricorn is posed with his foot under him and **his head is bowed, as if in death**. The second half of this symbol is the tail of the fish, the most prolific creature in nature, the fish lives in the waters, symbol of life and God's spirit. Out of the son of God's death, comes everlasting life.

-Capricornus is the modern Latin name of the sign, and means *goat.*

-There are 51 stars in the sign.

-The alpha star in the horn means the *goat.*

-The bright star in the tail means the *sacrifice that cometh.*

-Other star names mean: *the sacrifice slain; the record of the cutting off.*

 - **Aquarius**, the water bearer, the one pouring out life-giving waters that symbolize God's spirit, into the mouth of the fish. The beta star in the other shoulder=who goeth and returneth.

- **Pisces**, the fishes connected to the neck of the sea monster, **one points to the center of heaven the other follows the ecliptic**, the path of the earth around the sun. "Thy kingdom come, thy will be done on earth as it is in heaven."

- **Aries**, the lamb prepared from the foundations of the world, the unblemished sacrifice for mankind with his foot poised to strike off the tether attaching the fishes to the neck of the sea monster. "He (Jesus Christ), came to set the captives free."

- **Taurus**, the Bull. **His horns, symbolizing God's judgment**, are pointed to the earth, one stabs the heel of a shepherd "Aquilla", who holds his flock, Christ the good shepherd, received in our place God's absolute judgment. In the bulls neck in the Pleiades, the congregating of the judges, who come back to earth after their resurrection to judge the earth with Christ at his second coming.

## MESSIAH, THE COMING JUDGE OF ALL THE EARTH.

✓ The Hebrew name means both *coming* and *ruling*

✓ 141 stars

✓ The brightest star (in bull's eye) Al Debaran means the *leader*

✓ The star El Nath (at tip of left horn) means wounded or slain

✓ The cluster of stars (Pleiades) means congregation of the judges

- **Gemini**, the twins. Castor is the suffering redeemer, and Pollex is the king. Symbols of the first and second coming of Christ.

## MESSIAH'S REIGN AS PRINCE OF PEACE

✓ The Hebrew name means **united**. The Arabic name means the same.

✓ 85 stars

✓ Appollo means "ruler or judge".

✓ Bright star in other head means "who cometh to labor, or suffer"

✓ Star in left foot means "wounded".

- **Cancer**, the crab. **Originally it was the fortress, the impregnable enclosure of protection**. In Egypt it was a scarab, the beetle that hatched from the ground and flew to heaven, the stronghold of the saved.

- **Leo**, the great lion. "The conquering lion of Judah", Jesus Christ, who will come again. The king that the apostle John traced back to that tribe of Israel. **In his heart is the star called Regulus.**

This is the whole story of God's atonement work on earth; its beginning and ending are symbolized by the sphinx!

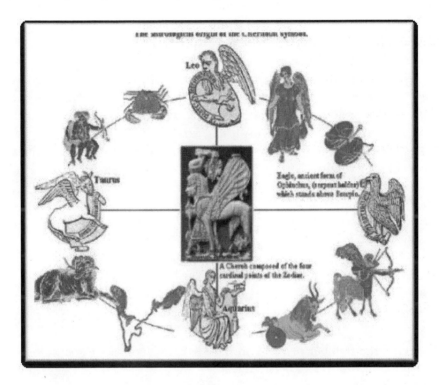

The Greek **myth Oedipus Rex contains symbols of relevance to corrupted truth.** When Oedipus encountered the Greek sphinx, he was asked a riddle. "What speaks with one voice, yet in the morning walks on four legs, walks at noon on two legs and in the evening walks on three legs?" Oedipus was the only man to answer correctly. The answer is "man." Upon hearing her riddle solved the sphinx screamed in rage, threw herself to the rocks below her lofty perch and died. Such a simple answer to this enigmatic question leaves one to ponder its significance.

What more can be gleaned from the content of the story? **The sphinx as it has been stated was actually a symbolic depiction of an angel.** This angel was not, however, anything like the dutiful messengers of God described in Scripture but a horrible monster bent on the destruction of any man it came in contact with.

At this point it will be helpful to understand some basic principles of the meaning of numbers in scripture. With insight into the symbolic meaning that numbers pose as they occur in the Bible one will understand the full meaning of the "Riddle of the Sphinx." The study of the meaning of numbers in scripture is called Biblical Numerics or Biblical Numerology. This book is intrinsic to theology and history of the Bible because of the language it was written in, Hebrew and Greek. These two languages share the aspect of using letters for words and also a system for counting. The spiritual meaning for numbers that continually show up in scripture, intentionally put there by God, can be discerned. The following list is a brief description of the symbolic meaning of primary numbers.

**One**: The symbol of unity, primacy and beginning, in all languages.

**Two**: The first number that can be divided from itself, it symbolizes division or difference.

**Three**: Is the number of the Trinity. It has the necessary dimensions for substance (length, breadth, & height).

**Four**: Represents the number for God; 3+1, the number of beginning. Thus four is the symbol of creation.

**Five**: Is 4+1, creation plus a new beginning. Five equals grace or favor. It should be said that 5 can also represent "death."

**Six**: Is the number of imperfection; the number of man. Creation plus division 4+2, or Grace with man's addition to it 5+1.

**Seven**: Is the number of completion. It is the number of spiritual perfection. Creation lasted six days, God rested on the seventh.

**Eight**: Is the number of resurrection; 7+1 is completion plus newness.

**Nine**: Symbolizes judgment. Akin to the number 6, six being the sum of its two factors (3+3=6); (3x3=9), it is significant of the end of man.

**Ten**: Symbolizes completeness of order. Ten is the number for Gentiles.

**Eleven**: If ten is that completeness of order, then eleven is the subversion and undoing addition to that perfect order.

**Twelve**: is the symbol of governmental perfection or rule (3x4); God's rule over His creation. There are 12 signs in the zodiac, 12 apostles, 12 tribes of Israel, 12 months in a year etc..

Returning to Oedipus Rex and the story of the sphinx, we find the symbolic types much more clear. **Oedipus, whose name literally means "wounded in the foot,"** was on his way to Thebes, the city of light. The king of Thebes had proclaimed that he would give the kingdom and the hand of his daughter in marriage, to anyone who destroyed the sphinx.

The earliest prophecy in the Bible concerning the redemption of fallen man is in Genesis: I will put enmity between you and the serpent. You will strike at his heel, and he will crush your head, ergo, wounded in the foot. If the numbers of the riddle are added together 1, 4, 2, & 3 the sum is 10; the number of perfection of order. If the numbers pertaining to walking on the earth before God are added together, the sum is 9, the number of judgment.

The sphinx, a symbolic angel, asked the question, "What speaks with one voice, yet walks on four feet in the morning, two feet at noon and three feet in the evening?" The question, decoded, should read like this: "What creature, spoken into creation by God, (1) walked before God in perfection at the beginning, (4) fell from grace and was divided from God, (2) and will be redeemed and made perfect by God (3)? The answer was man, but the real question hidden ingeniously in the riddle was this. Who will redeem man? What is his name?

**Figure 9 Eagle-headed Sphinx from Assyria**

**Figure 10 Persian Sphinx**

*Chapter 6*

# Star Gates

T he Great Pyramid of Giza is one of the seven wonders of the ancient world and the only one still remaining to this day. It is also called the Pyramid of Khufu and is the oldest and largest of the three pyramids in the Giza Necropolis. It is the oldest of the Seven Wonders of the Ancient World, and the only one to remain largely intact. The other wonders are: The Colossus of Rhodes, The Statue of Zeus at Olympia, The Mausoleum at Halicarnassus, The Hanging Gardens of Babylon, The Temple of Artemis (Diana) at Ephesus, and The Lighthouse of Alexandria.

Its construction demonstrates the remarkable insight of its placement on the face of the Earth. Joseph Seiss and others have demonstrated that the Pyramid lies in the center of gravity of the continents. It also lies in the exact center of all the land area around the world, dividing the earth's land mass into approximately equal quarters. The north-south axis (31 degrees east of Greenwich) is the longest land meridian, and the east-west axis (30 degrees north) is the longest land parallel on the globe. There is obviously only one place that these longest land-lines of the terrestrial earth can cross, and it is at the Great Pyramid! This is incredible, one of the scores of features of this mighty structure which begs for a better explanation. The Pyramid is at the earth's center!

The Great Pyramid of Giza stands on the northern edge of the Giza Plateau, located about 10 miles west of Cairo. It is composed of over 2 1/2 million blocks of limestone, which weigh from 2 to 70 tons each. Its base covers over 13 acres and its volume is around 90,000,000 cubic feet. You could build 30 Empire State buildings with its masonry. It is 454 feet high which is equivalent to a modern 48-story building. There are currently 203 courses or steps to its summit. Each of the four triangular sides slope upward from the base at an angle of 51 degrees 51 minutes and each side has an area of 5 1/2 acres. The joints between adjacent blocks fit together with optical precision and less than a fiftieth of an inch separates the blocks. The cement that was used is extremely fine and strong and defies chemical analysis. Today, with all our modern science and engineering, we would not be able to build a Great Pyramid of Giza. The Great Pyramid is thought to have been erected around 2600 BC during the reign of Khufu (Cheops). Next to the Great Pyramid stand 2 additional large pyramids. The slightly smaller one is attributed to Cheop's son and successor, Kephren. The other, still smaller, is attributed to Kephren's successor, the grandson of Cheops, Mykerionos. To the south-east of the Great Pyramid lies the Sphinx. The total number of identified pyramids in Egypt is about 80.

Some scientists today even claim that the works produced by the Egyptians—for whom, according to the evolution of history theses, the building of the pyramids must have been exceedingly difficult—were actually made by extraterrestrial visitors! This is known as the Ancient Astronaut Theory. Of course, any such claim is exceptionally irrational and illogical. Yet evolutionists hide behind it since all their demagoguery is unable to provide a better explanation. First and foremost, there is not the slightest evidence to support their claim. When evolutionists realize that they cannot produce any explanation based on chance or imaginary evolutionary process, they immediately hide behind the idea of "ETs from space." Indeed, they came up with this ridiculous idea when they realized that the DNA in the cell nucleus and the first protein, representing the fundamental building block of life, had far too complex and extraordinary structures to have arisen by chance from inanimate substances. And so, ETs from space must have brought the first living organism to the Earth and left it behind. This ridiculous claim is one of the telltale signs of the despairing position evolutionists find themselves in.

It also appears that the Great Pyramid was never finished since the top is flat, and not pointed, as it should be. It has a truncated summit which is coarse and uneven and measures about 30 square feet. Most pyramids were crowned with a top-stone that completed their structure. This pyramid does not currently have one and it appears that it never did. One of the earliest references to the missing top-stone (or capstone) is from Diodorus Siculus (60 BC). He tells us that in his day, when the Pyramid stood with its casing stones intact, the structure was "complete and without the least decay, and yet it lacked its apex stone." Since the top-stone could not have been dismantled without first demolishing the smooth casing stones, so that the core masonry formed steps of approach to it, this statement of Diodorus supports the theory that the top stone had never been added to the structure. Also it appears that between the different courses of stones there is a thin cement which is absent on the upper surface of the highest course. If ancient aliens built the pyramid, why did they not add the capstone to complete the pyramid? Nevertheless, why the pyramid was never finished remains a mystery.

Herodotus, the Greek historian of the fifth century BC, regarded as the father of history, wrote the earliest description in existence of the pyramids. When Herodotus visited them in 440 BC, it was as old to him as pyramids are to us! He wrote that each of the pyramids four faces were still covered with highly polished limestone (casing stones). Also the joints were so fine that they could hardly be seen. To manufacture just two blocks with a tolerance of 0.010 inch and place them together with a gap of no more than 0.020 inch is a remarkable feat. The Great Pyramid had at one time over 100,000 similar casing stones. Did the ancient Egyptians have advanced technology? The evidence suggests that they did.

It is safe to say that men have been seeking an answer to the riddle of the Great Pyramid for over 4,000 years. Theories range from a tomb or monument for a Pharaoh, an astronomical observatory, a place for elaborate Egyptian rituals, a giant sundial, a grain storage structure, a prophetic monument, a water irrigation system, a repository for ancient knowledge, the Egyptian Book of the Dead immortalized in stone, a communication device to other worlds or realms, etc. The list goes on. Also the list of who build the Great Pyramid includes the Egyptians, Sethites, Atlantians, and aliens to name a few. It is now known that ziggurats (the first pyramids) were associated with astrology and used for religious purposes.[31]

In the 14th century a series of earthquakes destroyed parts of northern Egypt. The Arabs decided to strip the pyramid of its casing stones to use in rebuilding bridges, mosques, palaces, etc. Eventually the pyramid was completely stripped of its beautiful casing stones and the core masonry was exposed to weathering. The core blocks proved to be of either pure limestone or nummulitic limestone containing large quantities of fossil shells resembling coins.

Any textbook on Egyptology will tell you that the pyramids were built as tombs for pharaohs. Why then is there so much interest about the Great Pyramid of Giza? Is there something unique about the pyramid? In the last 100 years, this assumption has been questioned for several reasons.

No mummy or remains of any kind have been found in the great pyramid. It does not seem likely that the pyramid had been robbed. When it was first entered by the Arabs in 820 AD, the only thing they found in the pyramid was an empty granite box in the King's chamber called the "coffer." (It is possible that there may have been one in the Queen's chamber also that has been destroyed since then.) Also, contrary to Egyptian practice, the empty lidless box was not inscribed nor decorated, for it would almost certainly have been covered with hieroglyphics and paintings had a pharaoh been in it. How many do we find? None!

---

[31] Ghirshman, Roman. "The Ziggurat of Tchoga-Zanbil" *Scientific American*, January 1961, pp.69-76.

It is the only pyramid in Egypt that has both descending and ascending inner passages. Otherwise, every other pyramid known has only descending passages. There must be some unique reason why this ascending passage with its chambers and magnificent grand gallery was built into the pyramid. We know that supposed airshafts were built into the King's and Queen's chambers, but what was the purpose of these airshafts? Dead pharaohs don't need air. There is so much detail and information built into the great pyramid that it seems it has another purpose.

When you study this information with an open mind, you realize that maybe this pyramid, the greatest one ever built, was not built as a tomb for a pharaoh, but for some other purpose. The pyramid is oriented true north with a greater accuracy than any known monument, astronomical site, or any other building. In our times, the most accurate north oriented structure is the Paris observatory. It is 6 minutes of a degree off true north. The Great Pyramid of Giza is only 3 minutes of a degree off true north. Studies have shown that this 3 minutes of a degree off true north is due to either a shift in the earth's pole or movement of the African continent. Originally it was perfectly oriented to true north. It was covered with casing stones (made of highly polished limestone). These casing stones reflected the sun's light. The pyramid shined like a star!

> The word *Pyramidos* has been translated as "Fire in the Middle"

In a recent PAX Cable Television Network Special that featured Christopher Dunn, the narrator stated that the origin of the word "pyramid" was unknown. Both academic Egyptologist and I would strongly agree this statement is incorrect, but I would strongly disagree with most Egyptologists on the true origin of the word. The word pyramid is derived from the Greek words *PYRAMIS* and *PYRAMIDOS*. The meaning of the word *Pyramis* is obscure and may relate to the shape of a pyramid. The word *Pyramidos* has been translated as "Fire in the Middle".[32]

---

[32] Stephen Mehler- the Land of Osiris Research Project.

Well known American Egyptologist Mark Lehner has stated that the ancient Khemitian term for pyramid was something he calls *MR. Pyramid*. Lehner bases this on his translation of *MR* as "Place of Ascension" following his belief that pyramids were tombs for kings and where the dead king's souls "ascended." But *MR*, usually written as *Mer*, is commonly translated as beloved, as in *Meriamen* (Beloved of Amen, The Hidden) or Meritaten (Beloved of Aten, The Wiser). Our indigenous sources tell us *Mer* meant "beloved" and had nothing to do with pyramid.

The ancient Khemitians used the term **PR.NTR, Per-Neter**, for pyramid. *Per* meaning "house" and Neter being translated by Egyptologists as "God" or Goddess" but we reject this mistranslation. In alignment with the indigenous tradition, we use the interpretation "House of Nature, House of Energy" for *Per-Neter*. The temple was *Per-Ba* (House of the Soul) and the tomb was *Per-Ka* (House of the Physical Projection) according to the indigenous tradition. With this understanding of *Per-Neter* as House of Nature, I state categorically that no one was ever intended to be buried in a pyramid in its original intent! Even Mark Lehner has admitted that no evidence of an original burial in any of the major Khemitian pyramids has ever been found. Also no inscription or reliefs either depicting or stating that any king was ever buried in a pyramid have been found.

One of the main purposes of the Great Per-Neter was to generate, transform, and transmit energy. The Indigenous Wisdom Keepers of Egypt have provided us a concrete paradigm to support the power plant theory of Christopher Dunn. Although Egyptologists base their pyramid-as-tomb theories on the writings of Greek historians such as Herodotus, the Greek word *Pyramidos* is closer to the true meaning. Indeed, if we support Dunn's ideas that the energy reactions in the Great Pyramid took place in the so-called Queen's and King's Chambers, then certainly it was Fire in the Middle!

It has been calculated that the original pyramid with its casing stones would act like gigantic mirrors and reflect light so powerful that it would be visible from the moon as a shining star on earth. Appropriately, the ancient Egyptians called the Great Pyramid "Ikhet", meaning the "Glorious Light!" How these blocks were transported and assembled into the pyramid is still a mystery. Many theories have been proposed, but none of them are really feasible.

When you look up at the Great Pyramid, its apex seems to be missing. It is a flat top not pointed like a pyramid should be. Usually, when a pyramid was constructed, the top part, or capstone (also called top-stone), was the last thing to be placed on it. It was considered the most important part of the pyramid and was made of special stone or even gold. The capstone was usually highly decorated. Was the great pyramid always without a capstone or was it stolen or destroyed? No one knows but the accounts of visitors to the pyramid from the ancient past (as far back as the time of Christ) always reported that the pyramid lacked a capstone. It is possible that it was never finished. Another possibility is that capstones were sometimes made of gold or maybe the first thing looted. The only problem is that this would be a very large capstone. If you climbed to the top, you could walk around very freely on the pyramid as many have done. It is about 30 feet in each direction. Thus, this capstone would have been huge and weighed a tremendous amount. Also on the summit you would see something that looks like a mast or flagpole. Actually it was placed there by two astronomers in 1874 to show where the Pyramid's actual apex would have been if finished.

On the back of the dollar bill, you can see a pyramid with a flat top. No one has been able to explain why the Great Pyramid would have been built without a capstone. As far as we know, the first people to enter the great pyramid since the time of Khufu were the Arabs in 820 A.D. Under caliph, Al mamoun, the Arabs broke into the great pyramid (since they could not find the hidden entrance) by boring into the limestone with crude instruments. After months they did manage to break in and find the descending passage. The connection of the descending passage with the ascending passage was blocked with granite plugs so they bored around these also. They finally reached the King's and Queen's chamber's and found nothing (except the empty granite box called "the empty coffin.") I have personally climbed inside the Great Pyramid to the King's chamber. There were no inscriptions, paintings, mummies, or treasures to be found.

We were taught that the pyramids were built around 2300 B.C. The blocks supposedly came from a limestone quarry miles away and over a period of 23-25 years the Egyptians built the pyramids. We will be looking at some things that tend to disprove this.

There are 3 pyramids together in the Nile Valley that are supposed to be burial places for 3 Egyptian kings. Some think that they built a ramp to come up on the pyramids, as they built them. You would need 10 feet of ramp for every foot in height.

**Figure 11 Author A.S. Judkins by the Pyramid of Khafre; the second-largest of the ancient Egyptian Pyramids of Giza.**

Now let's look at the layout of these pyramids. The great pyramid is made of 2.3 million blocks with a combined weight of 6 million tons. There are 203 courses of blocks going up to a height of 281 feet. The pyramid covers an area of 13.1 acres. The four sides of the pyramid face exactly the four directions of north, south, east, and west. Whoever built the pyramid had a purpose in laying it out so exact. The four corners of the pyramid are almost exact 90 degree angels.[33] The farthest corner off is

---

[33] Numbers were used in Ancient Egypt from very early times. Papyruses from 2,000 BCE describing mathematical problems have been found. The four most referred to documents are known as the Kahun fragments, and Berlin, Moscow and Rhind

only 3 minutes and 33 seconds of 1 degree off. The closest is only 2 seconds of 1 degree off. There are 60 minutes in each degree and 60 seconds in each minute. The apex of the pyramid comes out exactly over the center of the base. The limestone casing blocks have joints with a mean thickness of 20 thousandths of an inch. Those blocks vary from true square to one 1/100th of an inch!

We don't build things this exact anymore. Today, some doubt that before modern times, there was not enough knowledge to build the pyramids on purpose so precisely. It is laid out so exact on the meridian, that when the sun is directly overhead at high noon, no light falls on either the east or west wall. They absolutely knew the points of the compass.

This really goes against the grain of evolutionary theory, because we are supposedly at the pinnacle of evolution. There is no way they were supposed to know more than we know, right? Whoever built them also had knowledge of the stars and their movements. Someone is laying out a pyramid in the Nile Valley who has knowledge of: 1) Advanced Geometry; 2) Advanced Engineering; 3) Advanced Astronomy.

## ANCIENT ASTRONOMY

People living in Nabta Playa, a large basin in the Nubian desert , had by the 5th millennium  B.C. fashioned one of the world's earliest known  astronomical devices. Research suggests that it may have been an ancient "calendar" marking the summer solstice. Its first line of stones point to the brightest stars in Orion's belt and the second line of stones point to Sirius. The largest stone at Nabta Playa points to the brightest star in Orion- Betelgeuse.

---

papyruses. These documents state, with examples, the bases on which measurements are made. The Egyptians knew that a triangle whose sides measure 3:4:5 is a right triangle, and made use of this knowledge (which is now called the Pythagoras Theorem) in their construction calculations.

Alexander Badawy, and Virginia Trimble first recognized their astronomical significance was in the 1960´s. They suggested that the north shaft of the Great Pyramid's Queens Chamber aligned with "Beta" (B) in Ursa Minor, while the south shaft is aligned with Sirius. The constellation of Ursa Minor was only introduced in 600 BC. The Ancient Egyptians considered Ursa Major and Minor to be part of Draco (known to the ancient Egyptians as the Hippo. She was often associated with the goddess Hathor). Draco was associated with the goddess Tawret (who also took the form of a hippo). Sirius was associated with Isis and known as the "Nile Star" because of its annual appearance at sunrise on the day of the summer solstice. The southern shaft in the Kings Chamber is aligned with the Orion´s belt. Orion was associated with Osiris, a god of the netherworld. The northern shaft aligns with the star, Thuban, in the constellation of Draco.[34] These shafts are astronomical sightlines allowing the king's soul to reunite with the star-gods.[35]

According to some theorists, the alignment of the south shaft of the King's Chamber to Orion and the south Queen's Chamber to Sirius actually occurred much earlier that the Fourth Dynasty (2575 - 2465 BC), when the Great Pyramid is generally thought to have been built. Hence the argument that the Pyramid is much older than previously thought, and that the shafts may circumstantially support an earlier construction date.[36]

---

[34] Today, Polaris marks the North Pole, but at the time of the ancient pyramids, the star closest to the pole was Thuban. Thus it was of high astrological importance and considered to be a symbol of immortality (as it never left the night sky).

[35] There is some support for this in the Pyramid Texts, (which are dated to the fifth dynasty, but were most likely formed from earlier religious concepts), which make frequent references to the connection between the resurrection of the king and Sahu (Orion). This is in keeping with writings in the fifth dynasty which confirm that the king joins circumpolar stars which never rise or set. They turn around the north pole star (Thuban) without ever dipping below the horizon. The ancient Egyptians called them the "undying" stars.

[36] Proponents of this view often suggest that there was an advanced astrophysical ancient culture which built the great pyramid and then disappeared, along with its advanced ideas. This is not a new idea. Plato (428 to 347 BC) refers to an ancient

The Ancient Egyptians recognized Orion, and place it into their mythologies. They associate the stars of Orion with Osiris, the sun-god of rebirth and afterlife, and one of the most important gods of the ancient Egyptians.[37] The Pyramids at Giza align with Orion's belt and the supposed "air shafts" align to the constellation Orion and the Dog Star-Sirius (Sothis).

**Figure 12**

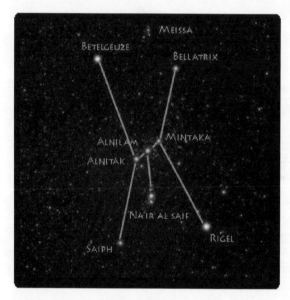

**Constellation of Orion**

Sirus is equated with the native Egyptian goddess Hathor (an ancient cow goddess) and also associated with Asherah worship in ancient Israel as well as Ishtar worship in Babylon. A significant fact is that Asherah's son is named "Baal".

Interestingly, Asherah is also known as the "Lion Lady"; two characters making up the Sphinx. In fact, artifacts have been discovered in the Sinai showing Asherah as a lion with a human female head! An artifact connecting Asherah in Israel to the Garden of Eden came in a discovery from the Sinai where she is identified as the "Lady of the Serpent!"[38&39] In the first millennium B.C. she was called "Chawat,"

---

culture whose knowledge was lost in "Timaeus," and Atlantis is still a remarkably popular idea.

[37] The Oxford Guide: Essential Guide to Egyptian Mythology, Edited by Donald B. Redford, p302-307, 2003. Berkley.

[38] Spencer, Peter, *The Davinci Cult*, 2006, BookSurge, pp. 34-35.

[39] The Gnostics worshipped the snake symbol. They did not see the snake as a seducer but rather as the liberator who brought knowledge to Adam and Eve by convincing

which is HAWAH in Hebrew and Eve in English! The memory of the ancients still connects Eve, the first goddess wannabe with Asherah. Asherah is ancient man's worship of their mother Eve![40]

The prophet Elijah fought not only against prophets of Baal, but also against "prophets of Asherah," indicating that the term could also be applied to an actual goddess as well as to a generic object of worship:

### 1 Kings 18:19-20 (KJV)
[19] Now therefore send, *and* gather to me all Israel unto mount Carmel, and the prophets of Baal four hundred and fifty, and the prophets of **Asherah** four hundred, which eat at Jezebel's table. [20] So Ahab sent unto all the children of Israel, and gathered the prophets together unto mount Carmel.

The prophet Jeremiah also vehemently opposed Asherah worship; the goddess called the "Queen of Heaven":

### Jeremiah 7:18 (KJV)
[18] The children gather wood, and the fathers kindle the fire, and the women knead *their* dough, to make cakes to the **queen of heaven**, and to pour out drink offerings unto other gods, that they may provoke me to anger.

Even ancient Israel went into idolatry worshipping Baal and the hosts of heaven in the high places.

---

them to eat of the Tree of Knowledge of Good and Evil and thus become as gods. Pantheism is the root belief system of the Gnostics.

[40] Spencer, Peter, *The Davinci Cult*, 2006, BookSurge, p. 35.

# Figure 13

The southern shaft from the Queens Chamber is aligned with the star Sirius. This star was associated with the mother Goddess Isis. The southern shaft emanating from the Kings Chamber aligned with the brightest star of the Orion Belt representing Osiris- the Egyptian God of resurrection and rebirth. The northern shafts aligned to the ancient pole star Alpha Draconis (Kings Chamber) and to Beta Ursa Minor (Queens Chamber).

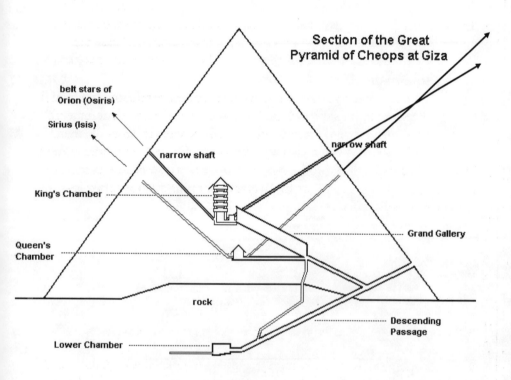

## 2 Kings 23:4-6 (KJV)

[4] And the king commanded Hilkiah the high priest, and the priests of the second order, and the keepers of the door, to bring forth out of the temple of the LORD all the vessels that were made **for Baal,** and **for the grove,** and **for all the host of heaven**: and he burned them without Jerusalem in the fields of Kidron, and carried the ashes of them unto Bethel.

[5] And he put down the idolatrous priests, whom the kings of Judah had ordained to burn incense in the high places in the cities of Judah, and in the places round about Jerusalem; them also that burned incense unto **Baal, to the sun, and to the moon, and to the planets, and to all the host of heaven.**

[6] And he brought out the grove from the house of the LORD, without Jerusalem, unto the brook Kidron, and burned it at the brook Kidron, and stamped *it* small to powder, and cast the powder thereof upon the graves of the children of the people.

These cultic sites of worship were often associated with high places[41], groves, or the cedars. It is important to know that Asherah's name literally translated means an actual grove of trees. Asherah's wooden pole is worshipped as the tree of life![42] These high places as seen in both Asherah and Baal cult practices were made as the physical & spiritual reflections of the original state of mankind before they lost the garden and consequently their fellowship with God.

---

[41] The Latin word for high is "alta", from which we get our word "altar".

[42] Side note: This can also include a stone pole (often phallic) of worship. India's Kateri people worship a stone and the Muslims also worship a stone in Mecca. In Hinduism, the word "ashram" may come from the root word; Asherah. Hindus still revere the cow as sacred! In our modern day vernacular, you still hear people use the term, "sacred cow."

## STELLAR ALIGNMENTS

"What is so special about the structures of stellar alignments? The nighttime sky played a crucial role in marking time in ancient Egypt. In *The Origin Map*, astrophysicist Thomas Brophy postulates that the arrangements of structures on the Giza plateau marked the location of the galactic center, the dense ball of stars around which the Milky Way's spiral arms rotate, at its northern culminations circa 10,909 B.C.[43] In *Galactic Alignment*, John Major Jenkins also found it evident that other ancient cultures were aware of this special stellar event and made it a part of their traditions. Indeed, for the Maya, it signaled the beginning of a new calendar and the ending of an old one; it is why their calendar ends in 2012, during a period of galactic alignment (and not the end of the world.) According to Jenkins, the constellation Leo is a critical marker for periods of galactic alignment. When it aligns with an equinox or solstice, either the axis of the solstice or equinox is aligned with the Milky Way and the galactic center."[44]

> Both the Babylonians and Egyptians worshipped the gods and built pyramids as high places where they could worship the stars (fallen angels) in their quest for immortality.

After the Great Noahic Deluge, Nimrod began to build a high place known as the Tower of Babel.[45] Nimrod's name means "let us rebel!"[46] This was probably a ziggurat designed to reach as high as they could into the heavens. Both the Babylonians and Egyptians worshipped the gods and built pyramids as high places where they could worship the stars (fallen angels) in their quest for immortality.[47] They were determined

---

[43] Brophy, Thomas. The Origin Map: Discovery of a Prehistoric, Megalithic, Astrophysical Map and Sculpture of the Universe (New York: Writers Club Press, 2002, pg.63.
[44] Malkowski, Edward, Before the Pharoahs: Egypt's Mysterious Prehistory, Bear & Co., 2006, pp. 294-295.
[45] The word "Babel" in its original Akkadian language means, "the Gate to God"!
[46] Morris, Henry. *The Defenders Study Bible*, note on Genesis 10:8 p.29
[47] This is called Astrology- used to foretell the future &/or worship the stars. This is different from the science of Astronomy.

to return to Eden wherein to recapture eternal life. We see this duplicated throughout different cultures such as the Chinese and the Mayans. According to Mayan mythology, the ancient ancestors of the Maya came "from the stars" to the four corners of the earth![48] One interesting note is that the Teotihuacan Pyramid in Mexico is the exact same base size as the Egyptian pyramid! On the outskirts of Mexico there is a Moon pyramid (symbolizing the good god) and the next to it the Sun pyramid (symbolizing the wife of God) surrounded by other smaller pyramids which have been found to represent the 10 original planets circling the sun.[49]

The original Garden of Eden was perceived by the ancients as the Gateway to God. After all, this is where Elohim walked among Adam and Eve. In Egyptian writings, they refer to the Nephilim as the "followers of Horus" and before that as simply "the gods." The pyramids are the star gates! The ancients were not only communicating the astronomical knowledge of the precession of the equinoxes, they were worshipping the fallen angels! Jesus' birth occurred between the constellations Aries and Pisces. Pisces, the fishes, connected to the neck of the sea monster, one points to the center of heaven the other follows the ecliptic, the path of the earth around the sun. "Thy kingdom come, thy will be done on earth as it is in heaven." Aries, the lamb prepared from the foundations of the world, the unblemished sacrifice for mankind with his foot poised to strike off the tether attaching the fishes to the neck of the sea monster. Jesus Christ came to set the captives free!

---

[48] These Ziggurat "high places" were reproduced around the globe on the same star line-the latitude band that connects the pyramids with the stars so they could behold the same stellar alignments!

[49] Spencer, Peter, *The Davinci Cult*, 2006, BookSurge, p. 233.

## Figure 14

### The locations of world's ancient sites on a global scale are on the same latitude (22.5 degrees in the ancient past).

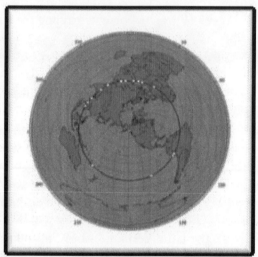

**MYSTERIOUS ALIGNMENT OF ANCIENT SITES OF THE WORLD**

The sites: Giza, Siwa, Tassili n'Ajjer, Paratoari, Ollantaytambo, Machupicchu, Nazca, Easter Island, Aneityum Island, Preah Vihear, Sukhothai, Pyay, Khajuraho, Mohenjo Daro, Persepolis, Ur, Petra are shown clockwise from Giza on the equal azimuthal projection. above. The projection is centered on the axis point in southeastern Alaska. Distances to any location from the center of an equal azimuthal projection are equally scaled. Since all of the sites on the great circle alignment are equally distant from the axis point at one quarter of the circumference of the earth, the alignment forms a perfect circle halfway between the center and the outer edge of the projection.[50]

---

[50] www.world-mysteries.com

## Chapter 7

# Forbidden History

The evolutionary picture of ancient man does not match the empirical evidence in fields such as archaeology nor in its historical context. Did you know that there is archaeological evidence confirming the biblical record? Or have you ever heard that the people described as "primitive cavemen" possessed an artistic ability and understanding just as refined as those of modern artists? Did you know that the Neanderthals, whom evolutionists portrayed as "ape-men," made houses, clothing, shoes, and took pleasure in music?

In all probability you may never have heard any of these facts. On the contrary, you may have been handed the mistaken impression that these people were half-ape and half-human, unable to stand fully upright, lacking the ability to speak words and producing only strange grunting noises. That is because this entire falsehood has been imposed on society for the last 160 years. The motive behind it is to keep alive an evolutionary philosophy which denies the existence of the Creator God of the Bible. According to this view, which distorts any fact that stands in its way, matter is eternal. In other words it had no beginning, and thus has no Creator. The supposedly scientific basis for this superstitious belief is the theory of evolution.

Since evolutionists claim that the universe has no Creator, they must provide their own explanation for how the life and myriad species on Earth came into being. The theory of evolution is the scenario they employ for that purpose. Before the Ancient Astronaut Theory, evolution suggested that all the order and life in the universe came about spontaneously by time and chance. Inanimate substances in the primeval world combined by accident to give rise to the first living cell. As a result of millions of years of similar coincidences, organisms came into existence. Consequently, human beings came on the scene, as the final stage of this supposed evolutionary chain. There are also those who hold to the Ancient Astronaut Theory suggesting that ancient aliens (extra-terrestrials) came to earth from other galaxies seeding their DNA into the human population and bringing advanced technology with them! This theory, known as "intelligent evolution" is an attempt to explain the causality of the complex design of life and living systems. What an oxymoron!

## THE COMPLEXITY OF LIFE

The primary reason why the theory of evolution ends up in such a dead end regarding the origin of life is that even those living organisms deemed to be the simplest have incredibly complex structures.[51] The cell of a living thing is more complex than all of our man-made technological products. Today, even in the most developed laboratories of the world, a living cell cannot be produced by bringing organic chemicals together.[52]

The conditions required for the formation of a cell are too great in quantity to be explained away by coincidences. The probability of proteins, the building blocks of a cell, being synthesized coincidentally, is 1 in 10,950 for average protein made up of 500 amino acids. In mathematics, a probability larger than $10^{50}$ is considered impossible in practical terms. In fact, there are just $10^{130}$ number of electrons in the known universe!

The DNA molecule, which is located in the nucleus of a cell and which stores genetic information, is an incredible databank. If the information coded in DNA were written down, it would make a giant library consisting of an estimated 900 volumes of encyclopedias consisting of 500 pages each.

---

[51] This principle is known as "irreducible complexity," an argument by proponents of intelligent design that biological systems are too complex to have evolved through the evolutionary means of natural selection.
[52] See Michael Behe's book, "Darwin's Black Box".

A very interesting dilemma emerges at this point: DNA can replicate itself only with the help of some specialized proteins (enzymes). However, the synthesis of these enzymes can be realized only by the information coded in DNA. As they both depend on each other, they have to exist at the same time for replication. This brings the scenario that life originated by itself to a deadlock. Prof. Leslie Orgel, an evolutionist of repute from the University of San Diego, California, confesses this fact in the September 1994 issue of the *Scientific American* magazine:

It is extremely improbable that proteins and nucleic acids, both of which are structurally complex, arose spontaneously in the same place at the same time. Yet it also seems impossible to have one without the other. And so, at first glance, one might have to conclude *that life could never, in fact, have originated by chemical means*[53] (emphasis added).

Usually the simplest explanation is the best. In science, this is known as "Ockham's Razor." In order to choose among these possible theories, a very useful tool is what is called Ockham's Razor. Ockham's Razor is the principle proposed by William of Ockham in the fourteenth century: "Pluralitas non est ponenda sine necessitate," which translates as "Entities should not be multiplied unnecessarily." In many cases this is interpreted as "keep it simple," but in reality the Razor has a more subtle and interesting meaning. Suppose that you have two competing theories which describe the same system, if these theories have different predictions... it is a relatively simple matter to find which one is better: one does experiments with the required sensitivity and determines which one give[s] the most accurate predictions.[54]

The simplest explanation for the origin of DNA, using the principle of Ockham's razor, is that it was designed- somewhat like a computer memory chip- and the original life-information was loaded into it by the designer.[55] No doubt, if it is impossible for life to have originat-

[53] Graham Hancock, Santha Faiia, Heaven's Mirror: Quest for the Lost Civilization, New York: Three Rivers Press, 1998, p. 304.
[54] http://physics.ucr.edu/~wudka/Physics7/Notes_www/node10.html
[55] Bates, G. Alien Intrusion, Master Books, 2004, p 129

ed from natural causes, then it has to be accepted that life was "created" in a supernatural way. This fact explicitly invalidates the theory of evolution, whose main purpose is to deny the Creator- the God of the Bible.

The early history of mankind—which is alleged to have come into being as the result of millions of accidental mutations, each more impossible than the last—has been distorted to fit in with this scenario. According to the evolutionists' account, the history of mankind is as follows: In the same way that life forms progressed from a primitive organism up to man, the most highly developed of all, so mankind's history must have advanced from the most primitive community to the most advanced urban society.

These concepts have now been falsified because of recent advances in science—particularly in the fields of biology, paleontology, micro-biology and genetics—have totally destroyed the claims of evolution.

Evolutionary scientists—in order to account for the supposed evolutionary process that they claim extends from a single cell to multi-celled organisms, and then from apes to man—have rewritten the history of mankind. To that end they have invented imaginary eras such as "The Cave-Man Age" and "The Stone Age" to describe the lifestyle of "Primitive Man." Evolutionists, supporting the falsehood that human beings and apes are descended from a common ancestor, have embarked on a new search in order to prove their claims. They interpret every stone, arrowhead or potsherd unearthed during archaeological excavations in that light. Yet the pictures and dioramas of half-ape, half-man creatures sitting in a dark cave, dressed in furs, and lacking the facility of speech are all fictitious. Primitive man never existed, and there never was a Stone Age.

These concepts have now been falsified because of recent advances in science—particularly in the fields of biology, paleontology, microbiology and genetics—have totally destroyed the claims of evolution. The idea that species evolved and transformed into "later" versions of each other, such as birds to dinosaurs concept, is an illogical conclusion. In the same way, human beings did not evolve from ape-like creatures. Human beings have been human since the day they came into existence, and have possessed a sophisticated culture from that day to this. Evolution never happened.

The evolutionist historical perspective studies the history of mankind by dividing it up into several periods, just as it does with the supposed course of human evolution itself. Such fictitious concepts as the Stone Age, Bronze Age and Iron Age are an important part of the evolutionist chronology.[56] Since this imaginary picture is presented in schools and in television and newspaper stories, most people accept this imaginary picture without question and imagine that human beings once lived in an era when only primitive stone tools were used and advanced technology was unknown.

Yet when archaeological findings and scientific facts are examined, a very different picture emerges. The traces and remains that have come down to the present—the pyramids, megaliths, artifacts such as tools, needles, flute fragments, personal adornments and decorations— show that in cultural and social terms, humans have had advanced ancient technology and civilizations without discernible periods of evolution.[57] This sudden onset of cultures possessing advanced technology 4,000 years ago is consistent with the Bible account after Noah's Flood, the proliferation of people in Sumeria and the scattering abroad of them during the Tower of Babel.[58] Omni magazine reported, "The unprecedented explosion of knowledge five thousand years ago, they believe, may have been foreshadowed by an earlier society whose cultural remnants have long since vanished."[59] Afterwards, the Sumerians, the Egyptians, and the Mayans all retained their technological knowledge to

---

[56] There are Biblical references of bronze being used in the Iron Age (I Samuel 17- the armor and weapons of Goliath) and iron being used in the Bronze Age (Canaanite Chariots Judges 1:19).

[57] Chittick, Don. *Puzzle of Ancient Man*, Creation Compass, 2006, pp.8-15

[58] Tower of Babel occurred in 2242 B.C. according to Archbishop Ussher's calculations using Genesis & Manetho's writings that this event occurred in the fifth year of Peleg's life.

[59] Robert Patton, "OOPARTS" *Omni*, Sept. 1982, p. 54.

build the same style-pyramids! But how could supposed primitive, stone age cultures develop complete and complex civilizations at the beginning? How did they learn the sciences? And where did they get their knowledge from? It certainly wasn't from ETs. We see the Nephilim at work once again imparting advanced knowledge to mankind.

Thousands of years ago, people lived in houses, engaged in agriculture, exchanged goods, produced textiles, ate, visited relatives, took an interest in music, made paintings, treated the sick, performed their acts of worship and, in short, lived normal lives just as they do today. Of course, throughout history, there have always been those living under simpler, more primitive conditions as well as societies living civilized lives.[60] But this by no means constitutes evidence for the so-called evolution of history, because while one part of the world is launching shuttles into space, people in other lands are still unacquainted with electricity. Yet this does not mean that those who build spacecraft are mentally or physically more advanced—and have progressed further down the supposed evolutionary road and become more culturally evolved—nor that the others are closer to the fictional ape-men. These merely indicate differences in cultures and civilizations.

## FORBIDDEN ARCHAEOLOGY

When you examine an evolutionist's history of mankind, you'll notice the detailed depictions of how man's allegedly primitive ancestors went about their daily lives. Anyone impressed by the confident, authoritative style, but without much knowledge of the subject, may well assume that all these "artistic reconstructions" are based on scientific evidence. Evolutionist scientists arrive at detailed descriptions as if they had been around thousands of years ago and had the opportunity to carry out observations. They say that when our supposed ancestors who had now learned to stand upright on two legs began making stone tools and for a very long period, used no other imple-

---

[60] Thomas, B. "'Primitive' Tribe Demonstrates Modern Social Behavior", ICR.org, 2 March 2012, http://www.icr.org/article/6721/

ments other than ones made of stone and wood. Only at a much later date did they start to use iron, copper and brass. Let's investigate this further.

In his book Archaeology: A Very Short Introduction, archaeologist Paul Bahn says that the scenario of mankind's evolution is nothing but a fairy tale, adding that so much of science is based on such tales. He stresses that he uses the word "tale" in a positive sense, but that still, this is exactly what they are. He then invites his readers to consider the traditional attributes of the so-called human evolution. How much of these conjectures, he wonders, are based on bones and actual remains, and how much on literary criteria? Bahn is reluctant to openly answer the question he poses: namely, that man's alleged evolution is based on "literary" criteria rather than scientific ones.

In fact, there are a great many unanswered questions and logical inconsistencies in these accounts, which someone thinking along the lines of evolutionist dogma will fail to detect. Evolutionists refer to a Stone Age, for example, but are at a loss to explain how winged insects first came to fly, though they maintain that dinosaurs grew wings and thus started to fly by trying to catch them. They prefer to invent scenarios to fill in the missing gaps of evolution.

Many archaeologists and scientists have performed tests to see whether such ancient artifacts could have been manufactured under the primitive conditions that evolutionists conjecture. For example, Professor Klaus Schmidt carried out one such experiment on the carvings on the stone blocks at Göbekli Tepe in Turkey.[61] He gave workmen stone tools, of the kind evolutionists claim were employed at the time, and asked them to produce similar carvings on similar rocks.

---

[61] Göbekli Tepe may be the oldest known human-made religious structure. It may predate Stonehenge & the Pyramids. The site is 300x300 meters large with some 20 stone endosures 30-100 ft. in diameter, depicting various animals within them. In the center of each endosure, are two 18ft. tall stone megaliths depicting faceless beings! This may indicate worship of the Nephilim (star people). The site has been under excavation since 1994 by German and Turkish archaeologists.

After six hours of non-stop work, all that the workmen managed to complete was one animal figure in bas-relief. To create all 16 enclosure stone bas-relief carvings for the entire site at the same rate would take some 12 months per enclosure. Yet, evidence suggests that people did not inhabit the site. Although archaeologists claim that Göbekli Tepe is in the Stone Age, it is more sophisticated than Stonehenge! The evidence should show primitive technology at this site. However, Göbekli Tepe is not a primitive site at all. It empirically demonstrates a high level of technology and organization to accomplish such a feat.

You can carry out a similar experiment at home. Take a piece of hard stone such as granite and try to turn it into a spearhead of the kind used by people *supposedly* living 100,000 years ago. But you are not allowed to use anything else than that piece of granite and a stone. How successful do you think you might be? Can you produce a piece with the same narrow point, symmetry, smoothness and polish as those found in the historical strata? Let me go even further; take a piece of granite one meter square and on it, try and carve a picture of an animal in bas-relief. What kind of result could you produce by grinding that rock with another piece of hard stone? Clearly, it is a difficult task.

Stone-cutting and stone carving are fields of expertise all their own. The requisite technology is essential in order to make files, lathes and other tools. This demonstrates that at the time these objects were made, the "primitive" technology was well advanced. In other words, evolutionists' claim that only simple stone implements were known during the Stone Age and that there was no advanced technology in existence. Indeed, a great many evolutionists now admit that archaeological findings do not support Darwinism at all.

Richard Leakey, an evolutionist archaeologist, admitted that it's impossible to account for the archaeological findings, especially stone tools, in terms of the theory of evolution:

"In fact, concrete evidence of the inadequacy of the Darwinian hypothesis is to be found in the archeological record." "Just one aspect of the prehistoric record is sufficient to show that the hypothesis is wrong: the record of stone tools."[62] However, in classifying history, evolutionists interpret the objects they find in line with their own dogmatic theories. The period during which bronze artifacts were manufactured they call the Bronze Age, and suggest that iron began being used much more recently—based on their claim that in the most ancient civilizations, metals were unknown. It's not logical to maintain that any society able to produce bronze was unaware of iron, that a society with the technical knowledge to produce bronze did not use any other metals.

Bronze is obtained by adding tin, arsenic and antimony, with a small quantity of zinc, to copper. Anyone who creates bronze must have a working knowledge of such chemical elements as copper, tin, arsenic, zinc and antimony, know at what temperatures these are to be melted, and possess a kiln in which to melt and combine them. Without all this knowledge, it will be very difficult to produce a successful alloy. You have to have a high degree of technology in order to do it.

To begin with, copper ore is found in old, hard rocks in powder or crystalline form (which is also referred to as "native copper"). A society that uses copper must first possess a level of knowledge to identify it in powder form in these rocks. It must then construct a mine to extract the copper, remove it, and carry it to the surface. It is clear that these things cannot be done using stone and wooden tools.

Copper ore must be introduced to red-hot flames in order for it to liquefy. The temperature needed to melt and refine copper is 1,984°F. There also needs to be a device or bellows to ensure a steady flow of air to the fire. Any society working with copper must construct a kiln able to produce such high heat and also make such equipment as crucibles and tongs for use with the furnace.

---

[62] Richard Leakey, *The Origin of Humankind* (Science Masters Series), New York: BasicBooks, 1994, p.12.

This is a brief summary of the technical infrastructure needed to work copper—which by itself, is too soft a metal to hold a sharp edge for long. Producing harder bronze by adding tin, zinc and other elements to copper is even more sophisticated, because every metal requires different processes. All these facts show that communities engaged in mining, producing alloys and metal-working must have possessed detailed

knowledge. It is neither logical nor consistent to claim that people with such comprehensive knowledge would never have discovered iron.

On the contrary, archaeological discoveries show that the evolutionist claim that metal was unknown and not used in very ancient

societies is untrue. Proof includes such findings as the remains of ancient metallic spheres, an iron hammer in Cretaceous rock,[63] and an iron pot in supposed 300 million years old coal![64]

## SUMERIAN SCIENCE

The Sumerians had their own number system. Instead of the present-day base-10 system (decimal), they constructed a mathematical system based on the number 60 (sexagesimal). Their system still occupies an important place in our own

---

[63] The chemical composition is 96.6% iron, 2.6% chlorine, & 0.74% sulfur. Chlorine fabricated with metallic iron remains a puzzling enigma. This iron oxide does not readily form under present environmental conditions. According to evolution, this artifact is in the same rock as the dinosaurs- supposedly 120 million years ago! Clearly, the geological dating is wrong. There are no eons of evolutionary time.
[64] http://manvsarchaeology.wordpress.com or http://aaronjudkins.com

day, in the way that we have 60 minutes in an hour, and 60 seconds in a minute, and 360 degrees in a circle. For these reasons, the Sumerians, whose mathematical knowledge produced the first geometrical and algebraic formulae, are regarded as the founders of modern mathematics.

The Sumerians attained a rather advanced level in astronomy, and their calculations of the years, months and days were almost exactly the same as ours. The Sumerian calendar, with its year consisting of 12 months, was also used by the Ancient Egyptians, the Greeks and a number of Semitic societies. According to this calendar, a year consisted of two seasons—summer and winter. Summer began on the vernal equinox, and winter on the autumnal equinox.

The Sumerians also studied the heavens from towers they referred to as "ziggurats."[65] Ziggurats were stepped pyramids- predating the Egypt's first pyramid! They were able to predict solar and lunar eclipses, as can be seen clearly in a number of records. To record their astronomical discoveries, the Sumerians made charts of a great many constellations of stars. In addition to the Sun and Moon, they also studied and noted the movements of Mercury, Venus, Mars, Jupiter and Saturn. The calculations that the Sumerians produced several thousand years ago have now been confirmed by the images sent back to Earth by spacecraft.

## THE NIMRUD LENS

A discovery made by the archaeologist Sir John Layard in 1850 raised the question of who actually used the first lens? During a series of excavations in what is now Iraq, Layard discovered a piece of a lens dating back 3,000 years. Currently on display in the British Museum,

---

[65] Samuel Noah Kramer, History Begins at Sumer: Thirty-Nine Firsts in Recorded History, Philadelphia: University of Pennsylvania Press, 1981.

this fragment shows that the first known lens was used in the days of the Assyrians. Professor Giovanni Pettinato of the University of Rome believes that this rock-crystal lens—which, according to him, is a major discovery shedding considerable light on the history of science—could also explain why the ancient Assyrians knew so much about astronomy, having discovered the planet Saturn and the rings around it. [66]

The ancient advanced societies made use of science and technology, built deeply-rooted civilizations and enjoyed advanced culture. Only limited information regarding their daily lives has come down to us today. In conclusion, none of these societies ever underwent evolution.

## THE BAGHDAD BATTERY

In 1938, the German archaeologist Wilhelm König discovered a vase-like object now known as the "Baghdad Battery." But how was it concluded that this object, some 2,000 years old, was used as a battery? If it actually was used as a battery—which the research carried out certainly indicates—then all theories to the effect that civilization always progresses and that societies in the past lived under primitive conditions, will be totally demolished. This clay pot, sealed with asphalt or bitumen, contains a cylinder of copper. The bottom of this cylinder is covered with a copper disk. The asphalt stopper holds in place an iron rod, suspended down into the cylinder, without making any contact with it.

If the pot is filled with an electrolyte, a current-producing battery is the result. This phenomenon is known as an electrochemical reaction, and is not far different from the way that present-day batteries work. During experiments, between 1.5 and 2 volts of electricity was generated by some reconstructions based on the Baghdad Battery.

---

[66] Dr. David Whitehouse, "World's Oldest Telescope?", BBC News, 1 July 1999, http://news.bbc.co.uk/1/low/sci/tech/380186.stm

This raises a very important question: What was a battery used for 2,000 years ago? If such a battery existed, then there also could have been advanced tools. This once again shows that people living 2,000 years ago possessed far more advanced technology—and by extension, living standards—than was previously thought.

## MEGALITHS

Megalith is the name given to monuments consisting of large blocks of stone. Many ancient megaliths have survived down to the present day. One of the most surprising aspects of these monuments is how such huge blocks of stone, some weighing more than a ton, were used to build the structures in question, how these stones were carried to their construction sites and by what techniques. How did the people of that time build these structures by placing one enormous block on top of another? These megaliths were generally built using stones brought from a long distance away, and are regarded today as marvels of construction and engineering. The peoples who produced such works must have possessed some advanced technology.

**Figure 15: Megaliths at Cusco. The stones fit so perfectly that not even a playing card can slide between them. There is no mortar. They often join in complex and irregular angles.**

Clearly, the people involved in constructing these monuments possessed knowledge and a technology far superior to what is generally imagined. Civilizations do not always move in a forward direction; sometimes it regresses. And indeed, most of the time, both advanced and primitive civilizations are able to exist simultaneously in different parts of the world.

It is probable that the people who constructed the megaliths possessed an advanced civilization, as evidenced by the archaeological sites such as Machu Picchu, Tiahuanaco, Baalbek, and Göbekli Tepe. The structures they produced show that they had a wide-ranging knowledge

**Did you know?**

The largest Inca stone at Cusco forms the corner of the saw-tooth wall of the lower terrace and weighs some 360 tons with a height over 27 feet!

of mathematics and geometry; that they knew the technology needed to build monuments by calculating fixed points in hilly areas; that they used equipment (such as the compass) to determine geographical positions, and that when necessary, they could transport the materials needed for construction from many miles away. Obviously, they could not manage all this by using only primitive tools. Indeed, many experiments by researchers and archaeologists have demonstrated that it would have been impossible to construct these monuments under the conditions proposed by the theory of evolution. Researchers who have attempted to construct similar monuments by reproducing the imaginary "Stone Age" conditions postulated by evolutionists have failed dismally. These researchers have not only found it difficult to construct any similar structure, but have also experienced enormous difficulties in transporting these stones from one place to another. This shows yet again that people of that era did not lead primitive lives, as evolutionists would have us believe. They understood architecture, made expert use of construction technology and engaged in astronomical investigations. On the basis of these megaliths, therefore, it is impracticable to make *interpretations* about the daily lives of societies of that time. Their social relationships, beliefs, tastes and artistic understanding cannot be deduced with any measure of certainty.

## NEWGRANGE

This monumental grave near Dublin is agreed to have been built around 3,200 BCE. Newgrange was already old at a time before Egypt's civilization had come into existence, and before the birth of Babylonian and Cretan civilizations. Stonehenge,

one of the most famous stone structures in the world, had not yet been built. Research has shown that Newgrange was not only a grave, but that its builders possessed a comprehensive knowledge of astronomy—and possessed engineering techniques and architectural knowledge worthy of emphasis.

A great many archaeologists describe Newgrange as a technical miracle. For example, the dome atop the structure is an engineering marvel all by itself. The single stones, heavy at the bottom and lighter on the upper parts, have been placed on top of one another so expertly that each one protrudes slightly from the one beneath it. From this, a hexagonal 19 ft. high chimney rises above the central part of the structure. On top of the chimney is a stone lid that can be opened or closed at will.

Obviously, this giant structure was built by people with an excellent understanding of engineering, able to calculate accurately, plan correctly, transport heavy loads of stone, and make good use of their construction know-how. Evolutionists can shed no light on how this structure was erected because, according to their unrealistic view, people of that time labored under primitive conditions. But it's impossible for such an enormous monument to have been built by anyone lacking a sophisticated knowledge of engineering and construction.

The structure's astronomical features alone are astonishing. This giant monument has been constructed in such a way that at winter solstice, it gives rise to an impressive light show. Shortly after daybreak on the shortest day of the year, a shaft of sunlight illuminates the Newgrange burial chamber. At this point, a perfect play of light occurs. Rays from the rising sun pass through a narrow opening on the bottom of the roof box over the entrance and shine down the passage to the inner chamber. All the stone blocks are placed at angles that allow the light to reach them and be reflected off them—one vital factor that makes this entire light show possible. You can see, therefore, that the builders of this giant structure not only had a knowledge of engineering, but also possessed a knowledge of astronomy that let them calculate the length of days and the movements of the Sun.

Newgrange is just one of many stone structures of that period surviving in that region. From looking at this structure, you can conclude that it was made by people with a deep accumulation of knowledge, using advanced techniques and methods.

## STONEHENGE

Stonehenge, a monument that stands in England, consists of some 30 large stone blocks arranged in a circle. Each of these blocks is an average of 15 feet high and weighs an average of 25 tons. The monument has attracted the attention of a great many researchers, and many theories have been proposed as to how and why it was erected. What matters here is not which (if any) of these theories is actually correct, but that this monument yet again invalidates the theory of "evolution" in the history of mankind.

Research reveals that Stonehenge was built in three main stages, beginning in about 2,800 BCE. In other words, scientist say the history of its construction goes back some 5,000 years! The initial stage of building included the digging of a ditch, bank and some round pits in the chalk. In the second stage, some 80 bluestones were set up in two rings around the center of the site and a heel stone was erected outside this. Later, an outer circle of giant stones was placed, with a continuous run of lintels.

One of the most noteworthy aspects of this monument is the bluestones used in it, because there are no sources of such stones anywhere nearby. These stones were imported to the site from the Preseli Mountains—some 240 miles away! If, as evolutionist historians claim, the people of that time lived under primitive conditions, with the only tools at their disposal being wooden cranks, timber rafts and stone axes, then how could they transport these stones all the way to the region where Stonehenge now stands? This question cannot be answered by scenarios that are mere figments of conjecture.

One group of researchers tried to transport bluestones as far as Stonehenge by reconstructing the equipment supposedly used at the time. To that end, they used wooden cranks, built a raft able to carry stones of an equivalent size by lashing three rafts together, moved the raft upriver using wooden poles, and then finally tried to move the stones uphill using crudely manufactured wheels. But their efforts were in vain. This was just one of the experiments carried out in order to establish how the bluestones might have been transported as far as where Stonehenge lies now. Many others have been performed, and investigators have attempted to understand what method of transportation the people of the time might have used. Yet none of these attempts came anywhere near achieving success, because they were all carried out under the misapprehension that the people who built Stonehenge had a primitive culture and used only crude implements made of stone and wood.

Another point that needs emphasis is that the experiments in question benefited from present-day technology. They used various models produced in naval shipyards; employed ropes produced in high-tech factories, and made detailed plans and calculations. Yet even so, they obtained no positive results. However, people living thousands of years ago transported these stones, weighing many tons each, and arranged them in a circle by calculating their exact geographical positions. Clearly, they did not accomplish all this with stone tools, rafts made of logs and cranks made of timber. Stonehenge and the many other megaliths were built using some technology we are unable even to guess at today.

## TIAHUANACO

At about 13,000 feet above sea level, in the Andes Mountains between Bolivia and Peru, the city of Tiahuanaco (Tiwanaku) is full of ruins that stun visitors. The region is regarded as one of the archaeological marvels of South America. The name Tiahuanaco literally means "the place where the observers dwell."

One of the most astonishing remains in Tiahuanaco is a calendar that shows the equinoxes, the seasons, and the position of the Moon at every hour and its motions. This calendar is one of the proofs that the people living there possessed a highly advanced technology. Among the other astonishing remains in Tiahuanaco are monuments made out of huge stone blocks; some of them weighing as much as 100 tons.

For example, the city walls were built by placing blocks weighing 60 tons on top of other blocks of sandstone weighing some 100 tons. The stone working used to build these walls required enormous expertise. Huge square blocks were joined together with accurate grooves. Holes 8 feet long have been opened in blocks weighing 10 tons. In some parts of the ruins, there are stone water conduits 6 feet long and 1.5 feet wide. These are of a regularity which is seldom equaled even today. It's impossible for these people to have produced these works in the absence of technological means, in the way that evolutionists claim. That is because under the allegedly primitive conditions, it would take longer than a human lifespan to produce just one of these structures. That in turn would mean that it took centuries to create Tiahuanaco, which alone shows that the evolutionist thesis is false.

### Figure 16 Gateway of the Sun

One of the most noteworthy monuments in Tiahuanaco is the so-called Gate of the Sun. Made out of a single block, it is 10 feet high and 16.5 feet wide and is estimated to weigh more than 10 tons. The gate has been decorated with various carvings. No explanation can be given as to what methods were used to construct the gate. What kind of technology was employed in the building of such an impressive structure? How were blocks of stone weighing 10 tons extracted, and by what means were they transported from the stone quarries? It is clear that all these things were achieved using more than just simple tools and equipment, of the kind alleged by evolutionists.

When you also consider the geographical conditions of the region where Tiahuanaco stands, the whole feat assumes even more astonishing proportions. The city is many miles away from any normal settlement areas and stands on a high plateau some 13,000 feet high, where atmospheric pressure is around only half that at sea level. A very interesting side note is a little known fact that Tiahuanaco was once completely under water![67] The monuments are covered in a thin layer of calcium. The greatly reduced oxygen level here would make tasks requiring a human workforce even more difficult. All this goes to show that, as in many other regions of the world, advanced civilizations existed here in the past—which invalidates the thesis that the societies always "evolve" towards more advanced states.

## THE MAYANS

The Mayans lived in Central America around 1,000 BCE, at a considerable distance from other advanced civilizations like those in Egypt, Greece and Mesopotamia. The most important features of the Mayans are the scientific advances they made in the fields of astronomy and mathematics, and their complex written language. They built highly developed cities, and who from the traces they left behind can be seen to have possessed a clearly advanced technology, calculated the orbit of the planet Venus and discovered the moons of the planet Jupiter. During this same era, people in many regions of Europe believed that the Earth was the center of the Solar System.

Three books which have come down to us from the Mayans, known as the Maya Codices, contain important information concerning their lives and astronomical knowledge. Of the three—the Madrid Codex, the Paris Codex and the Dresden Codex—the latter is the most important in terms of showing the depth of the Mayan knowledge of astronomy. They possessed a very complex system of writing, of which only less than 30% has been deciphered. Yet even this is enough to show the advanced level of science they attained.

For example, page 11 of the Dresden Codex contains information about the planet Venus. The Mayans had calculated that the Venus year lasted 583.92 days, and rounded it up to 584 days. In addition, they produced drawings of the planet's cycle for thousands of years. Two other pages in the codex contain information about Mars, four are about Jupiter and its satellites, and eight pages are devoted to the Moon,

---

[67] Kiss, Edmund. *Das Sonnentor von Tihuanaku und Horbigers Welteislehre*. Leipzig, Germany: Koehler & Amelang, 1937

Mercury and Saturn, setting out such complicated calculations as the orbits of these planets around the Sun, their relationships with one another, and their relationships with the Earth.

Mayan mythology refers to tall figures in white robes that came to the communities living in this region. According to the information contained on monuments, the Mayans believed in a single God but for only a short time before religious pluralism gave way. It was during this time that advances were made in their knowledge of the sciences.

## THE MAYAN CALENDAR

The Mayans' knowledge of time, astronomy and mathematics was a thousand years ahead of that of the Western world at the time. For example, their calculation of the Earth's annual cycle was a great deal more accurate than any other such calculations before the invention of the computer. The Mayans used the mathematical concept of zero a thousand years before its discovery by Western mathematicians, and used far more advanced figures and signs than their contemporaries.

The Haab, the civil calendar used by the Mayans, consisting of 365 days, is one of the products of their advanced civilization. Actually, they were aware that a year is slightly longer than 365 days; their estimate was 365.242036 days. In the Gregorian calendar in use today, a year consists of 365.2425 days.[68] As you can see, there's only a very small difference between the two figures—further evidence of the Mayans' expertise in the fields of mathematics and astronomy.

The year zero on the Mayan calendar was the creation of the world.[69] This year zero on the Mayan calendar agrees with the Biblical timeline. In fact, it agrees to within about fifty-six years of Ussher's famous chronology. It was 56 years shorter than the 4004 B.C. of Ussher! Other reliable historical records from other cultures, although pagan and

---

[68] The Mayan Calendar, http://webexhibits.org/calendars/calendar-mayan.html
[69] Morley, Silvanus, *The Ancient Maya*, Stanford University Press, 1956, p. 242.

supposedly having no knowledge of Genesis, also concur with the Genesis date of creation on 4004 B.C.[70]

So accurate was the Mayans' knowledge of astronomy that they were able to determine that one day needed to be subtracted from the Venus orbit every 6,000 years. How did they acquire such information? That is still a matter of debate for astronomers, astrophysicists and archaeologists. Today, such complex calculations are made with the help of computer technology. Scientists learn about outer space in observatories equipped with all kinds of technical and electrical apparatus. Yet the Mayans acquired their knowledge 2,000 years before the invention of present-day technology! This yet again invalidates the evolutionary theory that societies always progress from a primitive to a more advanced state. Many communities today have not yet achieved the levels attained by societies in the past. In short, civilizations sometimes move forwards and at other times regress. Nevertheless, both civilizations sometimes exist at the very same time.

What we have presented are only a few examples that demonstrate the advanced levels of civilization achieved by communities in the past. This points to one very significant truth; the evolutionary theory imposed for so many years, that societies in the past lived primitive lives is simply wrong. Societies with different levels of civilization and different cultures have existed in all ages; yet none evolved from any other. The fact that some primitive civilizations existed 1,000 years ago does not mean that history itself evolved, or that societies progress from the primitive to the more advanced. Because alongside these primitive communities, there were also highly advanced ones that made huge strides in science and technology and founded deep-rooted civilizations. Yes, cultural interaction and the accumulated knowledge handed down through generations may well play a role in societies' development. But this is not evolution.

When archaeological discoveries and the sites where past communities lived are examined, it can indeed be seen that most of these

---

[70] Cooper, Bill, *After the Flood: The Early post-Flood History of Europe*, New Wine Press, West Sussex, pp. 127-128.

societies enjoyed a higher level than some present-day communities, and that they made enormous advances in the fields of construction technology, astronomy, mathematics and medicine. This yet again invalidates the myth of evolution. Nevertheless, despite the empirical evidence against evolution, it prevails as the dominating theory of life origins. And it is the evolution connection that will play a key role in the future.

### FIGURE 17 THE MAYAN CALENDAR

*Chapter 8*

# The

# Evolution Connection

B ased on the theory of evolution, the search for extraterrestrial life has been carried out through radio astronomy. This is the listening to and studying of the characteristics of radio signals generated by both natural sources as well as unexplained sources in the universe. The first to suggest this method of contact with ETs was Nikola Tesla.

In 1992, NASA launched SETI, a 10 year, $100 million search for extraterrestrial intelligence. The centerpiece of SETI is the "Arecibo" radio telescope in Puerto Rico. The antenna dish is 1000 feet wide with power of over 20 trillion watts listening to over 15 million radio channels.

John Billingham, former project director of SETI, admitted that the US wants to be the first nation to make contact.

## UFO ORIGIN THEORIES

Here are the possible explanation theories of UFOs:

1. God could have created intelligent life on other planets and one or more of these technologically advanced life forms are now visiting us here on planet Earth.

2. Still others believe there are life forms from other planets, but they have evolved and were not created by God at all.

3. What people are seeing are really angelic manifestations from God. God is using his angels to give us vital information and prophecies.

4. What people are experiencing is demonic and associated with the fallen Angels.

5. People are only seeing things which have a rational, earthly explanation.

## UFO MESSAGES

People sometimes claimed to have been in contact with alien life forms. Often through an occultic means, messages are sent to those who "open themselves" up to the messengers. In Whitley Strieber's book, Communion, he describes having multiple alien abductions. When he asked about their identity they replied in short that they could not reveal their "true" identity. Strieber compares the "familiar" being he sees, whom he describes as female, to the Sumerian goddess- Ishtar. Strieber said:

> "I felt an absolutely indescribable sense of menace. It was hell on earth to be there [in the presence of the entities], and yet I couldn't move, couldn't cry out, couldn't get away. I lay as still as death, suffering inner agonies. Whatever was there seemed so monstrously ugly, so filthy and dark and sinister. Of course they were demons. They had to be. And they were here and I couldn't get away."[71]

That statement carries more truth than most people would like to admit. What about their message? It's one of apparent help and concern for mankind. Literally thousands of mediums and UFO contactees claim that they have received messages from "Mr. Ashtar" in recent years. "Ashtar" or "Ashtaroth" or "Asherah" was the name of a female deity of

---

[71] Missler, C. and Eastman, M. "Alien Encounters", Koinonia House, 1997. pg. 148

the Canaaanites in biblical times.[72] On one account, here is one such message from "Ashtar"; a supposed extraterrestrial:

*Our rescue ships will be able to come in close enough in the twinkling of an eye to set the lifting beams in operation in a moment. And all over the globe where it events warrant it, this will be the method of an evacuation. Mankind will be lifted, levitated shall we say, by the beams from our smaller ships. These smaller craft will in turn taxi people to the larger ships overhead, higher in the atmosphere, where there is ample space and quarters and supplies for millions of people.*

It goes on to say that the evacuation is for millions of people who are "out of tune" with Mother Earth. Here is another message:

*Humanity is learning a great lesson at this time. The lesson is, of course, to realize your Godhead, your connectedness with the prime creator and with all that exists. The lesson is to realize that everything is connected and that you are part of it all.*

Lastly, *Your history has been influenced by a number of the light beings whom you have termed God. In the Bible, many of these beings have been combined to represent one being, when they were not one being at all, but a combination of very powerful, extraterrestrial light being energies.*

Now back to Whitley Streiber. On another occasion in 1998 he had a very strange encounter with a "man" who knocked on his hotel door. Streiber awoke from his sleep to answer the door. The "man" stood motionless at his doorway talking about various subjects ranging from science to technology. As the stranger spoke, Strieber took notes, eventually privately publishing the first edition of his book, "The Key," two years later, in 2000. After 45 minutes, Streiber asked a very odd question during the encounter. He asked, "What is sin?" The stranger replied, "Sin is denial of the right to thrive."[73] Afterwards, the stranger gave him something that looked like "milk," wherewith Streiber took it

---

[72] Wilson, C., UFO's & the Mission Impossible, Signet, 1974, pp 94-95
[73] Retrieved on April 1, 2012.
http://www.huffingtonpost.com/2011/09/07/communion-author-whitley-strieber_n_943681.html

immediately and drank it. Immediately, he fell asleep. Whatever that was, it sealed Streiber's unholy communion.

It's interesting to hear that definition of the word sin. It clearly isn't a biblical one. That definition gives anyone the authority to do "what thou wilt." I was a teenager in High School when I learned the actual biblical definition of sin. Although I was a Christian from age seven, I did not know how to define sin. It was through my HS English teacher that gave me the correct definition. He asked me to define sin as a result of a paper that I had written for a class assignment. I wrote mine on something to the effect of morals and how to discern right from wrong. But I could not define the word sin in which I wrote. When the teacher asked me to define the word, I replied with a series of answers, "It's when you do something you're not supposed to do"; "when you do something wrong" I continued. I clearly remember to this day when he told me the correct definition. He said, "Aaron, sin is separation from God." The light bulb came on instantaneously! I have never forgotten that moment in my life. It is through the redefining of a word that changes the entire original intent, meaning, or message.

**1 Timothy 4:1-2 (KJV)**
[1] Now the Spirit speaketh expressly, that in the latter times some shall depart from the faith, giving heed to seducing spirits, and doctrines of devils;
[2] Speaking lies in hypocrisy; having their conscience seared with a hot iron;

If these are messages from ETs, how did the ETs get here? And why are they so secretive and elusive about it? Maybe these messages aren't from ETs in the distant cosmos. After all, no alien space craft is ever seen entering or leaving Earth's atmosphere. These are not friendly ET's here to help mankind. They are hyper-dimensional beings; malevolent in nature and demonic in origin.

## BEYOND THE FOURTH DIMENSION

We live in a 4 dimensional universe; length, width, height. What is the 4th dimension? Time! Most people overlook that dimension. If we take spaces with more than three *spacial* dimensions we call them "hyper-spaces" (this is also known as "string theory" in quantum physics). It may be that these hyperspaces may hold the key to understanding the strange phenomena being observed with UFOs. They seem to be hyper-dimensional!

Indeed, there are some problems with the interplanetary theory. Most experts doubt that the UFO's are really from other planets. However, they seem to be deliberately posing as such. The tremendous distances and the speed required would make such travel next to impossible-regardless of how technologically advanced the life form.

The next closest galaxy to us on earth is 2 million light years from Earth. That is, traveling at the speed of light (186,282.0244866 miles per second) it would take at least 2 million years to make the trip. Our nearest star is Alpha Centari some 4.5 light-years away. Traveling at 1,000,000 miles/day, it would take 70,000 years to make the journey! Not only are we talking about vast distances but according to a leading astrophysicist, Simhony has shown that space travel at even 1% of the speed of light (3,000km/s) ionization dissociation occurs! At 1,000km/s metal begins to dissolve and at a mere 100km/s the body temperature rises to *beyond* 40°C causing hyperthermia then death.[74]

No one has ever been able to explain how it is that a space ship to travel the vast distances that exist between galaxies. If they traveled all that way, then why are they just making brief, repetitive visits? Where are they between sightings? To further illustrate, imagine a spaceship carrying 10 passengers traveling 5 light years to and from a nearby star system at 70% of the speed of light. The estimated fuel consumption would be equal to 500,000 times the energy used in the US in one year. Not only is there a problem with distances and fuel and time, but there are other facts that argue against intelligent beings from other planets visiting Earth: not one UFO has ever responded to radio signals or any other communication from Earth. Space is not a vacuum. It is full of dust, debris, gas and particles like one hydrogen atom per cubic centimeter. Traveling at near light speed would produce in one square yard the

---

[74] M. Simhony, Matter, Space, Radiation, Hebrew University, 1990, p. 91A

equivalent radiation as produced by several hundred atom-smashers. This is a huge shielding problem. Physical beings are subject to physical laws regardless of their technology. This would make interstellar travel all but impossible. Life did not evolve on this planet nor did it on millions of others.

Another argument against UFOs being from other planets lies is the large number of sightings. Most sightings take place after 6 PM with the activity beginning to peak at 10:30 PM, reaching its height at midnight and trailing off in the predawn hours. The point is that UFO activity is nocturnal by nature. If most people weren't in bed at night, the sightings would be even higher. Also, both landings and sightings are in sparsely populated areas. What does all this mean? The encounters are far more numerous than required for any physical survey of the planet, so that is not what is taking place. We will expand on this later as we discuss what UFOs are here to do.

UFOs have been seen all through history and have received their own explanation within the framework of each culture. The UFOs seem to remain consistently one step ahead of human technology. For example, in antiquity, UFO occupants were "gods," in the ninth century UFOs were seen as "the vessels in the sky," in medieval times UFOs were seen as magicians or dragons, in the 19th century they were seen as scientific geniuses, and then our own time as interplanetary travelers. The UFOs have always adapted themselves to the technological capacities of the observers.

Another factor that argues against the extraterrestrial theory is the super physics of the UFOs. Extreme acceleration and deceleration, right angle turns while traveling at thousands of miles per hour, absence of sonic booms, the ability to materialize and dematerialize are but a few of the standard features of UFOs. In other words, UFOs don't always behave like material objects are to behave. UFOs cannot be explained within a natural context. That means that we must then look to the supernatural or spiritual context. So let's examine the supernatural theories:

## SUPERNATURAL THEORY #1

God could have created intelligent life on other planets one or more of which have become technologically advanced enough to visit Earth. This theory may be possible but it doesn't make any sense. Couple this with the fact that the Bible makes no mention of life created anywhere other than on earth in this theory is unlikely. When the Bible speaks of the eternal kingdom being set up, it always has the earth as the governmental Center. Is that supposed to be the reward for being the most "backward" civilization?

## SUPERNATURAL THEORY #2:

This suggests that UFOs are angelic manifestations. We can rule out the idea that the occupants of UFOs are angels in heaven since the channeled messages that are claimed to be received are very often unbiblical in nature. Plus, while the UFO occupants are described by abductees as small or short, this does not fit with the description of biblical angels. Plus, no Angel needs a vehicle for transportation and needs not to conduct any research on the earth, vegetation or humans. There are other differences as well, which we will examine later.

## Supernatural theory #3:

The 3rd supernatural theory is that UFOs are a demonic phenomena. It seems convenient to me that Christians automatically ascribed everything to the devil and his cohorts. And at times in history, that unfortunately, has been the case. But there is something to this theory which bears investigation. There is a consistent similarity between the messages and the behavior of the demonic in the UFOs.

People today can't get enough of the paranormal. That is why there are TV shows that feature a host or hostess that seems to have the ability to communicate with the dead, passing messages to people in the audience. When we see that the host dresses nicely and is articulate, he or she seems to be a "good person," the tendency is to forget what is actually taking place here. After all, it's on TV isn't it? People love to see the host come up with information that he couldn't possibly have known on his own. That is all that is needed to convince most that there is real communication with departed loved ones. After all, he is just trying to bring some comfort to these audience members, he's not hurting anyone. Or is he? Could it be that this is just one more way to acclimate a person to receive anything that appears to be legitimate without evaluating it from the word of God?

## THE PANSPERMIA THEORY

The Panspermia theory comes from a Swedish professor of physics, Savante Arrhenius (1859-1927). It is based on the theory of evolution. Since evolution cannot explain the origin of life[75], this theory says that life was seeded from outside our galaxy somewhere in the cosmos. It is really a hypothesis that life exists throughout the Universe, possibly distributed by meteoroids, asteroids, planetoids, or now even by ETs to the Earth. This is the basis of cosmic evolution.

Just as life supposedly evolved on Earth, life must have also evolved on other planets, some to a point more advanced than life on our planet. This theory includes the idea that all UFOs are visits by extraterrestrials. Most of the UFO researchers support this theory.

When Darwin put forward his theory in the middle of the nineteenth century, he never mentioned how the origin of life, in other words the first living cell, came to be. Scientists looking for the origin of life at the beginning of the twentieth century began to realize that the theory was invalid. The complex and perfect structure in life prepared the ground for many researchers to perceive the truth of creation. Mathematical calculations and scientific experiment and observation demonstrated that life could not be the "product of chance," as the theory of evolution claimed.

With the collapse of the claim that coincidence was responsible and the realization that life was "planned," some scientists began to look for the origin of life in outer space. The best-known of the scientists who

---

[75] The Law of Biogenesis- Life can only come from life.

made such claims were Fred Hoyle and Chandra Wickramasinghe. These two cobbled together a scenario in which they proposed that there was a force which "seeded" life in space. According to the scenario, these seeds were carried through the emptiness of space by gas or dust clouds, or else by an asteroid, and eventually reached the Earth, and life thus started here.

Nobel Prize–winner, Francis Crick, co-discoverer with James Watson of the double helix structure of DNA, is one of those who has sought the origin of life in outer space. Crick came to realize that it is quite unreasonable to expect life to have started by chance, but he has claimed instead that life on Earth was started by intelligent "extraterrestrial" powers.

As we have seen, the idea that life came from outer space has influenced prominent scientists. The matter is now even discussed on the History Channel series, "Ancient Aliens" along with numerous others on the origin of life.

The key to evaluating the "life began in outer space" theory lies in studying the meteorites that reached the Earth and the clouds of gas and dust existing in space. No evidence has yet been found to support the claim that celestial bodies contained non-earthly creatures that eventually seeded life on Earth. No research that has been carried out so far has revealed any of the complex macromolecules that appear in life forms. Furthermore, the substances contained in meteorites do not possess a certain kind of asymmetry found in the macromolecules that constitute life. For instance, amino acids, which make up proteins, which are themselves the basic building blocks of life, should theoretically occur as both left- and right-handed forms ("optical isomers") in roughly equal numbers. However, only left-handed amino acids are found in proteins, whereas this asymmetric distribution does not occur among the small organic molecules (the carbon-based molecules found in living things) discovered in meteorites. The latter exist in both left- and right-handed forms.[76]

"Considerable disagreements between scientists have arisen about detailed evolutionary steps. The problem is that the principal evolutionary processes from prebiotic molecules to progenotes have not been proven by experimentation and that the environmental conditions under which these processes occurred are not known. Moreover, we do not actually know where the genetic information of all living cells originates, how the first replicable polynucleotides (nucleic acids) evolved, or how the extremely complex structure-function relationships in modern cells came into existence."[77]

That is by no means the end of the obstacles to the theory that bodies and substances in outer space gave rise to life on Earth. Those who maintain such an idea need to be able to explain why such a process is not happening now, because the Earth is still being bombarded by meteorites. However, study of these meteorites has not revealed any "seeding" to confirm the thesis in any way.

Another question confronting the defenders of the theory is this. Even if it is accepted that life was formed by a consciousness in outer space, and that it somehow reached Earth, how did the millions of species on Earth come about? That is a huge dilemma for those who suggest that life began in space. Alongside all of these obstacles, no trace has been found in the universe of a civilization or life form that could have started life on Earth. No astronomical observations, which have picked up enormous speed in the last 30 years, have given any indication of the presence of such a civilization.

---

[76] Massimo Pigliucci, Rationalists of East Tennessee Book Club Discussion, October 1997

[77] Dose, Professor Dr. Klaus, "The Origin of Life; More Questions than Answers," Interdisciplinary Science Reviews, vol. 13, no. 4 (1988), pp. 348-356. Dose is Director, Institute for Biochemistry, Johannes Gutenberg University, West Germany. p. 348

The truth in question is that a theory that seeks to explain life on Earth as being the result of chance is no longer tenable. In fact, the areas of expertise of the scientists who sought the origin of life in outer space give a clue as to their rejection of the logic of the theory of evolution. Scientists such as Hoyle, Wickramasinghe, and Crick began to consider the possibility that life came from space because they realized that life could not have come about by chance.

According to the Panspermia theory, the first life formed not on Earth, but on some other planet. These organisms were subsequently carried to Earth in the form of spores or seeds by meteors, and life thus began here. However, current knowledge shows that it is impossible for spores or seeds in the irradiated vacuum of space to have withstood the heat, pressure, dangerous rays, etc. through their journey to Earth.

Therefore, the claim that the first life formed on another planet does not resolve evolutionists' problems at all, but merely places them one step back. The obstacles to life emerging by chance on Earth will also apply on any other planet. As we have seen, the theory that life on Earth was begun by extraterrestrials has no scientific basis to it. No discoveries have been made to confirm or support it.

## THE EVOLUTION CONNECTION

In the 1980's, the actress Shirley MacLaine gleefully announced a shocking proclamation in front of a large television audience. She stood with open arms on the shore of the Pacific Ocean and shouted, "I am God, I am God, I am God!"[78] This was a planned act for the popularization of the New Age movement. What Mrs. MacLaine may or may not know is that that title of "I AM" is already taken! And there is only one person that holds that specific title. He is the I AM of the Old Testament-the God of Abraham, Isaac, and Jacob.

### Exodus 3:13-14 (KJV)
[13] And Moses said unto God, Behold, *when* I come unto the chil-

---

[78] This was shown in the television mini-series "Out On a Limb" in 1987.

dren of Israel, and shall say unto them, The God of your fathers hath sent me unto you; and they shall say to me, What *is* his name? what shall I say unto them?

[14] And God said unto Moses, I AM THAT I AM: and he said, Thus shalt thou say unto the children of Israel, I AM hath sent me unto you.

## John 8:58 (KJV)

[58] Jesus said unto them, Verily, verily, I say unto you, Before Abraham was, I am.

Today, this teaching preaches that everything is God and God is all- that God and nature are one. In other words, every person is God! From this comes the conclusion in which reveals one's latent divinity; to recognize oneself as "god." When one finally understands your divine nature," say the 'apostles' of the New Age doctrine, a remarkable sensation will overcome you that you are above space and time; above all that is material.

However shocking this may be, this boastful belief is not new. Similar proud statements are declared by Hinduism which has preached them for eons of time. A modern advocate of Hinduism, Sai Baba, writes, "You are the God of the universe... You truly are God ... You are not man, you are God."[79] During transcendental meditation, you are to believe that "I am the sun; I am the true, true sun... The whole universe moves by me and receives its existence from me... I was before the beginning of the world... I penetrate every atom and bring it into movement... Oh, how marvelous I am... I am the entire universe... Everything is in me... I am God!"[80] This is absolutely ludicrous, pious, boastful, and prideful just to name a few. Such claims are an abomination to God.

Mormonism is another example of this. Here's what the Mormons preach: "As man is, God once was. As God is, man may be-

---

[79] Sathyam-Shivam Sundaram; Sathya Sai Speaks, Bangalore, India, 1973.
[80] Swami Visnudevananda, The complete Illustrated Book of Yoga, New York, Pocket Books, 1972.

come."[81] Also, "remember that God our heavenly Father was perhaps a child, and mortal like we are, and rose step by step in the scale of progress, in the school of advancement; has moved forward and overcome until He has arrived at the point where He is now."[82] Joseph Smith, the founder of the sect of Mormons, preached, "I am going to tell you how God came to be God. We have imagined and supposed that God was God from all eternity. I will refute that idea, and take away the veil, so that you may see .... It is the first principle of the gospel to know for a certainty the character of God, and to know that we may converse with him as one man converses with another and that he was once a man like us; yea, that God himself, the Father of all [of] us, dwelt on an earth..."[83]

Similar statements are made by other Mormon "prophets." Jesus Christ is not the Second Person of the Holy Trinity, but rather one of the gods, equal with the angel Lucifer and with other spirits! This is tragic that people have yielded themselves to the sin of pride, under which one can proclaim to be god. The apostle Paul stated that a distinctive characteristic of the antichrist will be his boundless pride. This will be **"that man of sin, the son of perdition, who opposeth and exalteth himself above all that is called God or holiness, so that he will sit in the temple of God as God, portraying himself that he is God" (2 Thes. 2:4).**

Edward Meier, a Swiss farmer, claims to have had hundreds of contacts with aliens. His main contact, a female humanoid, told Meier that she comes from a race of beings in the star group Pleiades. They are here she says, to guide us into spiritual and technical knowledge.

It is important to note that any doctrine exalting man at the expense of the Creator is of **occult origin.** This is known as pagan polytheism with its magic and mysteries, as well as Mormonism which is dictated by "spirits;" which has introduced a corrupted gospel. The apostle Paul warns us of this in Galatians. These theosophical teachings, such as Hinduism, Buddhism and the New Age movement also preach

---

81 Lorenzo Snow, Millennial Star, vol. 7 and vol. 54.
82 Orson Hyde, Journal of Discourses, vol. 1.
83 J. Smith, *Teachings of the Prophet Joseph Smith,* pp. 345-347.

pantheism. Rejecting the Creator God of the Bible, they teach that nature itself is Divine.

### Galatians 1:7-9 (KJV)

[7] ... there be some that trouble you, and would pervert the gospel of Christ.

[8] But though we, or an angel from heaven, **preach any other gospel unto you** than that which we have preached unto you, let him be accursed.

[9] As we said before, so say I now again, If any *man* preach any other gospel unto you than that ye have received, let him be accursed.

Even though this passage specifically refers to the preaching of the gospel of the kingdom in the dispensation of grace, the "false gospels" circulating today certainly "pervert the gospel of Christ" and are worthy of the same condemnation.

## THE GREATEST HOAX ON EARTH

I am convinced that the theory of evolution, and the extent to which it's been applied, is one of the greatest deceptions in history!

Those who believe in the theory of evolution think that a few atoms and molecules thrown into a huge vat could produce thinking, reasoning professors and university students; such scientists as Einstein and Galileo; such artists as Humphrey Bogart, Frank Sinatra and Luciano Pavarotti; as well as antelopes, lemon trees, and carnations. Moreover, as the scientists and professors who believe in this nonsense are educated people, it is quite justifiable to speak of this theory as "the greatest hoax in history." Never before has any other belief or idea hidden the truth from people as if they had been blindfolded. In fact, God has pointed to this lack of reason in the Bible.

**2 Timothy 4:2-4 (KJV)**

$^2$Preach the word; be instant in season, out of season; reprove, rebuke, exhort with all longsuffering and doctrine.

$^3$For the time will come when they will not endure sound doctrine; but after their own lusts shall they heap to themselves teachers, having itching ears;

$^4$And they **shall turn away** *their* **ears from the truth, and shall be turned unto fables.**

Words cannot express just how astonishing it is that the lie of evolution should hold the entire world enthralled to keep people blinded from the truth. Today, the mystery of iniquity continues to blind people to the Truth. I am convinced that the theory of evolution, and the extent to which it's been applied, is one of the greatest deceptions in history! It is used to confuse the world about the origin of life and the nature of mankind. In the New Age paradigm, man is either a product of blind evolution or the result of alien genetic manipulation through "intelligent evolution." However, it is impossible to accept such a theory with increasing evidences of a young universe[84] and the complex yet delicate balance required for life against all odds.[85]

But a greater deception is coming and people who miss the Second Coming of Christ will find themselves in a different time period; living out the Book of Revelation. That future is not far off. It is important to note that any doctrine exalting man at the expense of the Creator is of **occult origin.** This is known as pagan polytheism with its magic and mysteries, as well as Mormonism which is dictated by "spirits"; which has introduced a corrupted gospel. The apostle Paul warns us of this in Galatians. These theosophical teachings, such as Hinduism, Buddhism and the New Age movement also preach pantheism. Rejecting the Creator God of the Bible, they teach that nature itself is Divine.

> We find that every issue connected with the UFO phenomena centers around evolution and Bible prophecy.

---

[84] Morris, J., *The Young Earth*, Master Books, 1994
[85] Baugh, C., *Against All Odds*, Hearthstone Publishing, 1999

Do you see the connection? We find that every issue connected with the UFO phenomena centers around evolution and Bible prophecy. The lie is that the authority of the sky people or aliens from outer space will come to "help" mankind from destroying himself. They are here to save the world! Mankind will accept them because they have a superior intelligence than men.

It is extremely likely that the alien agenda is that these ETs will soon visit Earth in plain view and divulge their next evolutionary goal for mankind. It is unknown at this time if the Antichrist will use this tactic, but he may indeed use the UFO phenomena to usher in the New World Order. The New Agers of today believe that out of some future global disturbance or chaos, there will be a quantum leap in metaphysical consciousness.

I believe this is the Evolution Connection. If cosmic evolution can be "verified" outside our known galaxy, this will seem to embolden the Ancient Astronaut Theory. However, this is the deception that they will perpetrate. They are malevolent hyper-dimensional beings that are involved in the great cosmic battle for mankind's eternal soul! And they will use it to usher in the New World Order that will lead us down a path of destruction the world has never known. It will be worse than the prior two World Wars combined!

This is more than a scientific debate, it's a spiritual battle. We utterly reject the evolutionary hypothesis. The alien agenda to guide man to a higher spiritual development is a complete deception and total rejection of the true God- the God of the Bible. The sci-fi era has desensitized our society to the possibility of paranormal feats and when the ETs come, mankind will accept them at face value. This will be part of the great coming delusion.

*Chapter 9*

# The Coming Delusion

M ake no mistake about it. There is a coming delusion that will be so great that people during the End Times will buy into THE LIE- hook, line, and sinker. The great delusion which is coming is the Antichrist. There will be global world governance and a new religious system set up directed by the false prophet that will throw the world into the New World Order (NWO). And it is coming and at an alarming speed!

### Daniel 8:23-25 (KJV)
23 And in the latter time of their kingdom, when the transgressors are come to the full, a king of fierce countenance, and understanding dark sentences, shall stand up.
24 And his power shall be mighty, but not by his own power: and he shall destroy wonderfully, and shall prosper, and practise, and shall destroy the mighty and the holy people.
25 And through his policy also **he shall cause craft to prosper in his hand**; and he shall magnify *himself* in his heart, and by peace shall destroy many: he shall also stand up against the Prince of princes; but he shall be broken without hand.

### 2 Thessalonians 2:9-12 (KJV)
9 *Even him*, whose coming is after the working of Satan with all power and signs and lying wonders,
10 And with all deceivableness of unrighteousness in them that perish; because they received not the love of the truth, that they might be saved.

[11]And for this cause **God shall send them strong delusion, that they should believe a lie**:
[12]That they all might be damned who believed not the truth, but had pleasure in unrighteousness.

The "lie" of vs. 12 has to do with the "son of perdition" exalting himself as God. He will bolster this deception with "lying signs and wonders (vs. 9). Carl Sagan, believed in cosmic evolution due to his belief in a Big Bang and the fallacy of evolution. Yet in calculating the odds that life could evolve on just *one planet*, he estimated it to be roughly one chance in ten followed by two billion zeros![86] In other words, it is not just improbable, it's impossible! Nevertheless, Sagan, NASA, and the New Age believe that if evolution occurred on earth, it must have occurred elsewhere in this enormous universe.[87]

There are also many UFO cults like the Raelians who believe that life on Earth was "created" by intelligence from elsewhere. For example, they credit the aliens for the creation of the unbelievably complex information written on DNA molecules that are found in all living things on Earth.[88] The Lie will include "scientific" verification of UFO or alien contact. This delusion will be so strong using the Alien Agenda that people will believe in cosmic evolution when official contact is made from a superior race of ETs who are supposedly benevolent and will help us accomplish our next stage of evolutionary progress. They will oversee mankind as we advance to our next stage of evolution; not a physical one; but a spiritual one. That we should become gods-just like them! Believing the Lie will lead a person to accept the Antichrist as a savior of the world. The Bible also says that they will also take pleasure in all unrighteousness.

---

[86] Wilson, C. & Weldon, J., Close Encounter: A Better Explanation, Master Books, 1978, p 322

[87] Bates, G. Alien Intrusion, Master Books, 2004, p35

[88] Ibid, p 37

**Romans 1:28-32 (KJV)**
[28] And even as **they did not like to retain God in** *their* **knowledge**, God gave them over to a reprobate mind, to do those things which are not convenient;
[29] Being filled with all unrighteousness, fornication, wickedness, covetousness, maliciousness; full of envy, murder, debate, deceit, malignity; whisperers,
[30] Backbiters, haters of God, despiteful, proud, boasters, inventors of evil things, disobedient to parents,
[31] Without understanding, covenantbreakers, without natural affection, implacable, unmerciful:
[32] Who knowing the judgment of God, that they which commit such things are worthy of death, not only do the same, but have pleasure in them that do them.

No longer will the world tolerate the Christian faith and the Bible. It will deny the Truth and accept the Lie. The first thing to get suppressed in any lie is the truth. The very best way to not be deceived is to know the truth. A lot of strange things are yet to happen on this earth. Many of them are in the Tribulation. That deception will include the Son of Perdition. When the Holy Spirit is removed, the mystery of iniquity will culminate in the revelation of the man of sin; the Antichrist.

**2 Thessalonians 2:3-8 (KJV)**
[3] Let no man deceive you by any means: for *that day shall not come*, except there come a falling away first, and that **man of sin** be revealed, **the son of perdition**;
[4] Who opposeth and exalteth himself above all that is called God, or that is worshipped; so that he as God sitteth in the temple of God, shewing himself that he is God.
[5] Remember ye not, that, when I was yet with you, I told you these things?
[6] And now ye know what withholdeth that he might be revealed in his time.
[7] For the **mystery of iniquity doth already work**: only he who now letteth *will let*, until he be taken out of the way.
[8] And then shall that Wicked be revealed, whom the Lord shall consume

Now there are some things we need to know before we see how the world was in the days of Noah. Where will the Antichrist come from?

**Revelation 11:7 (KJV)**
[7] And when they shall have finished their testimony, **the beast that ascendeth out of the bottomless pit** shall make war against them, and shall overcome them, and kill them.

**Revelation 17:8 (KJV)**
[8] The beast that thou sawest was, and is not; and shall ascend out of the bottomless pit, and go into perdition: and they that dwell on the earth shall wonder, whose names were not written in the book of life from the foundation of the world, when they behold the beast that was, and is not, and yet is.

There are some pretty wild things in that bottomless pit and some of those things will be unleashed upon the world. Now we understand that the Beast (the Antichrist) will come from the bottomless pit!

**Revelation 9:1-11 (KJV)**
[1] And the fifth angel sounded, and I saw a star fall from heaven

unto the earth: and to him was given the key of the bottomless pit.

[2] And he opened the bottomless pit; and there arose a smoke out of the pit, as the smoke of a great furnace; and the sun and the air were darkened by reason of the smoke of the pit.

[3] And there came out of the smoke locusts upon the earth: and unto them was given power, as the scorpions of the earth have power.

[4] And it was commanded them that they should not hurt the grass of the earth, neither any green thing, neither any tree; but only those men which have not the seal of God in their foreheads.

[5] And to them it was given that they should not kill them, but that they should be tormented five months: and their torment *was* as the torment of a scorpion, when he striketh a man.

[6] And in those days shall men seek death, and shall not find it; and shall desire to die, and death shall flee from them.

[7] And the shapes of the locusts *were* like unto horses prepared unto battle; and on their heads *were* as it were crowns like gold, and their faces *were* as the faces of men.

[8] And they had hair as the hair of women, and their teeth were as *the teeth* of lions.

[9] And they had breastplates, as it were breastplates of iron; and the sound of their wings *was* as the sound of chariots of many horses running to battle.

[10] And they had tails like unto scorpions, and there were stings in their tails: and their power *was* to hurt men five months.

[11] And they had a king over them, *which is* the angel of the bottomless pit, whose name in the Hebrew tongue *is* Abaddon, but in the Greek tongue hath *his* name Apollyon.

Ok. Now back to the Antichrist. I believe he will take advantage of the belief in cosmic evolution and make his appearance in a UFO. Why?

- What nations would accept a world leader from another country?

- He will have to have a way to explain those lying signs and wonders; which includes calling down fire from heaven.

- It is the perfect way to lay the groundwork to "be a god."

Now let's sum up what we have so far.

1. The mystery of iniquity is already at work.

2. There is an invasion coming from out of this world.

3. I believe we can identify what is behind the UFO phenomena.

4. The UFO phenomena has occultic qualities. (Eastern and New Age religion is promoted while Jesus Christ is not.)

5. The messages are unbiblical.

6. While Christians should be knowledgeable, they should not get hooked up with the UFO agenda.

7. There is a cloud of death, called the "shadow of death" that will fly over the earth during the tribulation and kill people it passes over with radiation.

## THE SHADOW OF DEATH

We are going to look at Psalms 23 which is read practically at every funeral for a spiritual application. But we have totally missed the doctrinal application of the psalm which lands it in the tribulation. Historically, David is speaking of God's deliverance from his enemies. The reason for reading Psalm 23 is to pick up the phrase "shadow of death".

**Psalm 23:1-6 (KJV)**
[1] The LORD *is* my shepherd; I shall not want.
[2] He maketh me to lie down in green pastures: he leadeth me beside the still waters.
[3] He restoreth my soul: he leadeth me in the paths of righteousness for his name's sake.
[4] Yea, though I walk through the valley of the *shadow of death*,

I will fear no evil: for thou *art* with me; thy rod and thy staff they comfort me.

⁵ Thou preparest a table before me in the presence of mine enemies: thou anointest my head with oil; my cup runneth over.

⁶ Surely goodness and mercy shall follow me all the days of my life: and I will dwell in the house of the LORD for ever.

When we run references to the shadow of death, the first one that shows up is in Job 3. First we need a little background about the book of Job.

- You should know that every verse in the Bible has three applications: spiritual, doctrinal and historical.

-Job has a ton of prophetic material which is doctrinally related to the Great Tribulation.

-Job has 42 chapters-one for each month of the Great Tribulation.

### Matthew 24:21 (KJV)
²¹ For then shall be great tribulation, such as was not since the beginning of the world to this time, no, nor ever shall be.

Let's look at Job 2.

Job is on the ground seven days and nights, one day for each year of Daniels 70th week.

### Job 2:13 (KJV)
¹³ So they sat down with him upon the ground seven days and seven nights, and none spake a word unto him: for they saw that *his* grief was very great.

The word "Job" means "one persecuted." This is exactly what Israel will be in the Tribulation. Job is in Edom, exactly where Israel will be in the Tribulation. The same one who persecutes Job [Satan, the

Dragon] will persecute Israel in the tribulation.[89] So because Job's tribulation is a type of Israel's tribulation, then it would naturally occur that Job's "captivity" is restored at the end of the book, just like Israel's.[90] There is only one man who is said to have his "captivity turned" and that is Job. This is too big to overlook as a coincidence! The indicator is that Job is a type of Israel in the tribulation.

If you want to get the low down on the Antichrist, then go to the book of Job.

→ Descriptions of the antichrist and the devil

→ movements of troops in the Tribulation

→ landmarks for the 2nd Advent

→ the condition of Israel at the time

→ post-tribulation plagues

→ Demon-worship during the tribulation

→ references to the 2nd Advent (the second coming of Christ)

Now with that, let's continue.

> **Job 3:5 (KJV)**
> [5] Let darkness and the *shadow of death* stain it; let a cloud dwell upon it; let the blackness of the day terrify it.

---

[89] CF: Job 1:6-9 & Revelation 12:13

[90] CR: Job 42:10, Psalm 126:1, Jeremiah 29:14, Zephaniah 3:20.

### Jeremiah 13:15-16 (KJV)

[15] Hear ye, and give ear; be not proud: for the LORD hath spoken.

[16] Give glory to the LORD your God, before he cause darkness, and before your feet stumble upon the dark mountains, and, while ye look for light, he turn it into the **shadow of death**, *and* make *it* gross darkness.

### Amos 5:8 (KJV)

[8] *Seek him* that maketh the seven stars and Orion, and turneth the **shadow of death** into the morning, and maketh the day dark with night: that calleth for the waters of the sea, and poureth them out upon the face of the earth: The LORD *is* his name:

These "seven stars" may be a reference to the 7 stars of the Pleiades or the seven planets that were so well known to the ancients. These would be Venus, Mars, Jupiter, Saturn, Neptune, Mercury, and Pluto. Uranus was not discovered until 1781. However, something is wrong with the catalog of planets for seven are well known by all the ancients while the eighth seems to be a newcomer.

Now for those of you who think the shadow of death is only some conversation about dying, look at the following reference.

### Job 12:22 (KJV)

[22] He discovereth deep things out of darkness, and bringeth out to light the **shadow of death**.

Who didn't already know about dying? Since when was dying such a "new thing" that God had to unveil this great truth for people to discover? What great "light" did God shed on the "shadow of death" in the time Job was written? One more time, with gusto!

### Job 34:19-22 (KJV)

[19] *How much less to him* that accepteth not the persons of princes, nor regardeth the rich more than the poor? for they all *are* the

work of his hands.

$^{20}$ In a moment shall they die, and the people shall be troubled at midnight, and pass away: and the mighty shall be taken away without hand.

$^{21}$ For his eyes *are* upon the ways of man, and he seeth all his go-ings.

$^{22}$ *There is* no darkness, nor **shadow of death**, where the workers of iniquity may hide themselves.

Now why would a man think he could hide in the darkness? Why would a worker of iniquity think he could hide in the shadow of death unless it was a place of refuge for him?

### Job 24:17 (KJV)

$^{17}$ For the morning *is* to them even as the shadow of death: if *one* know *them, they are in* the terrors of the **shadow of death**.

### Job 38:17 (KJV)

$^{17}$ Have the gates of death been opened unto thee? or hast thou seen the doors of the **shadow of death?**

We didn't even use all the references, including Job and Psalms. And we didn't use any of the "shadow of death" references in Amos, Isaiah, Jeremiah, Matthew or Luke. But this is enough. You can run the references yourself on the shadow of death. And when you get to Job 38:17 you should get the cross reference in Job 36.

### Job 36:27-33 (KJV)

$^{27}$ For he maketh small the drops of water: they pour down rain according to the vapour thereof:

$^{28}$ Which the clouds do drop *and* distil upon man abundantly.

$^{29}$ Also can *any* understand the spreadings of the clouds, *or* the noise of his tabernacle?

$^{30}$ Behold, he spreadeth his light upon it, and covereth the bottom of the sea.

$^{31}$ For by them judgeth he the people; he giveth meat in abun-dance.

$^{32}$ With clouds he covereth the light; and commandeth it *not to shine* by *the cloud* that cometh betwixt.

[33] The noise thereof sheweth concerning it, the cattle also concerning the vapour.

Let's see what we have learned about these clouds in the above passage.

1. The ordinary clouds that are over your head may contain something other than dust and vapor. They may shield UFOs.

2. The ordinary clouds over your head may be connected with interstellar observation by the principalities and powers of Ephesians 6:11-13

3. There is a constant association of clouds with nearly every major event in biblical history and it is not accidental.

→ Gen 9- the Flood

→ Exodus 14; Exodus 19 - the giving of the Law

→ Exodus 40 - the Tabernacle

→ Job 3 - the shadow of death

→ Job 22 - a covering for the Lord as He walks in the heavens

→ Job 26 - the throne and the heavens are covered

→ Job 30 - they are terrors

→ Ps. 18 - his secret place

→ Ps. 104 - the clouds are His chariots

→ Daniel 7- the 2nd Advent

→ Zeph. 1- the Tribulation

→ Luke 9 - Mt. of Transfiguration, not to mention the crucifixion and the ascension.

4. Clouds are connected in some way with God's judgments on people or a country (Job 36:31)

5. Invisible UFOs may have learned to bend light rays long before the U.S. Navy experimented with the matter in World War II.

6. The "noises" in the passage are not merely "lightning" and clouds; they are the "noise of His Tabernacle" (vs 29) and His Tabernacle" is clearly the universe! (See Exodus 25).

The Tabernacle that was made according to the pattern of the things in the universe! The Tabernacle is primarily a picture of the 1st, 2nd, and 3rd heavens (Hebrews 8-10) and the data missing in Genesis 1 and Job 38 can be found in Exodus 25-30 and Exodus 35-39! It would take a Bible-believing mathematical genius to work out the material found in Exodus 25-30. It would take a solid five years or more of work in Exodus alone to work out the doctrinal content that Hebrews 8 and 9 indicate.

7. The bright light of 36:15 and 37:15 cannot be lighting, for men see not the "bright light which is in the clouds." That would be some "bright light" you've got there if no one can see it! Here is the thought that splits into possible explanations for UFOs.

This is where the coming great delusion will deceive many in the last days. The antichrist will lead mankind into the next "evolutionary" step to a spiritual evolution and make the same bold & prideful declaration, "Ye are gods!" Lucifer's original lie, "Ye shall not surely die" is exactly opposite of what the Creator had said, "Thou shalt surely die." Somebody is lying.

The temptation before Adam and Eve has two parts. First, the temptation was for them to believe that they had the right to decide who was telling the truth, the Creator, or some other source. Secondly, the temptation was for them to believe that they were smart enough to tell who was telling the truth, the Creator or some other source... In effect, one must be God.[91] Chittick continues,

"At the time of the Fall, man tried to elevate himself to the status of God. He wanted to decide for himself what was true or not true, instead of submitting to the absolutes of the Creator. Since that time, mankind has been in rebellion against the Creator. As a result, people tend to justify their rebellion. There are two approaches that people use. Either one will think his way into a pattern of living; or one will live his way into a pattern of thinking." "By pretending that we weren't created, man could therefore delude himself into believing that he was autonomous and not morally responsible to a Creator. He could live his way into a pattern of thinking and could generate his own standards of what is right and wrong and set his own standards for truth. Satan's lie is that man will not die and that they could attain deity and all knowledge, whereby becoming a perfect being. Instead, mankind fell into a terrible abyss of sin and thus lost their position in the Garden."

The devil's lie is that man would not die and that they could attain deity and all knowledge becoming perfect. Instead, mankind fell into a terrible abyss of sin and thus lost their position in the Garden. By pretending that we weren't created, man could therefore delude himself into believing that he was autonomous and not morally responsible to a Creator. He could live his way into a pattern of thinking (the lie of evolution) and could generate his own standards of what is right and wrong and set his own standards for truth.[92]

## LUCIFER'S POLICIES BEHIND THE PLAN OF EVIL

Satan does have a plan. In fact, some of you may have even read about that plan without knowing what you were reading. The Satanic plan of evil is that Satan will become the possessor of heaven and earth. His campaign slogan (if I can call it that) is that he is better suited than God to be the possessor of heaven and earth and all creatures would

---

[91] Chittick, Donald. The Puzzle of Ancient Man, Creation Compass, 1998, pp. 23-24.
[92] Ibid, p. 25

rather live in his kingdom than God's. Would you like to see where Satan stated his goal outright? Take a look at Isaiah 14.

> **Isaiah 14:12** How art thou fallen from heaven, O Lucifer, son of the morning! how art thou cut down to the ground, which didst weaken the nations!
> 13 For thou hast said in thine heart, **I will** ascend into heaven, **I will** exalt my throne above the stars of God: **I will** sit also upon the mount of the congregation, in the sides of the north:
> 14 **I will** ascend above the heights of the clouds; **I will** be like the most High.

You may have heard of the 5 "I wills" of Satan listed here. The first four of them constitute the successive steps that must be taken in order to achieve the 5th "I will" which is his final objective. When Satan says he will be like "the most High," he knows what that title means. That is the title given to the "possessor of heaven and earth." To see this, let's turn to Genesis where Abraham meets Melchizedek. Notice how the title, "most high God," is defined in the passage as the "possessor of heaven and earth."

> **Genesis 14:18** And Melchizedek king of Salem brought forth bread and wine: and he was the priest of the most high God. 19 And he blessed him, and said, Blessed be Abram of the most high God, possessor of heaven and earth:

> **Genesis 14:22** And Abram said to the king of Sodom, I have lift up mine hand unto the LORD, the most high God, the possessor of heaven and earth,

Lucifer, before man was created, achieved the usurpation of the heavens, by convincing the principalities to join with him. Now why is this important to know? It is important because through 23 of the 24 principalities joining the satanic rebellion against God, Satan became the "prince of the power of the air." That leads us to the why that is important, which is, by that title, Satan has achieved one half of his stated goal in the His plan of evil.

When man falls in the Garden of Eden, Satan becomes the "de facto" possessor of the earth. This was his goal all along and once he has achieved a measure of it, his desire is to hang onto it permanently. The rest of everything that follows in the Bible, including the activity of the sons of God in Genesis 6, the Flood that destroyed the world, the call of Abraham, the Exodus out of Egypt, the tower of Babel, all the way through to the judgments in the book of Revelation (and everything in between) is the record of what has taken place (and will take place) in the battle between God and Satan over who will be the possessor of heaven and earth. And how you live your life gives testimony as to which kingdom you would rather live in. You should stop and think about that for a moment. That is the storyline that connects all the seemingly unconnected stories in your Bible. And they are not just there for amusement or entertainment, but they are there for a purpose.

When you see that Satan is trying to hang on to what he has usurped possession of, it sheds some light on the events that have happened in this world, not only in biblical times but even today. Also, Satan's policies have some (perverted) genius to them. We should say a word about the difference between the satanic plan of evil and Satan's policy of evil. The "plan" is to be possessor of heaven and earth. The policies are the steps he implements to achieve that. Therefore, his policies change with the change in dispensations. So this strategy of having some of the angels cohabit with human women has an added secret benefit.

Do you remember that right after Adam and Eve took of the tree of the knowledge of good and evil, God made a promise of a coming "seed." This was a promise of a Messiah that would come to redeem men.

**Genesis 3:15** And I will put enmity between thee and the woman, and between **thy seed** and **her seed**; it shall bruise thy head, and thou shalt bruise his heel.

The things to notice about this verse are:

- There is a seed of the serpent which is the Antichrist
- There is a seed of the woman which is the Messiah
- The seed of the serpent will bruise the heel of the seed of the woman
- The seed of the woman will bruise the head of the seed of the serpent
- The "heel" of the Messiah is bruised at Calvary – a heel bruise being a minor wound in comparison to the head wound (deadly wound) given to the seed of the serpent
- The head of the seed of the serpent is bruised at the Armageddon Campaign when the Lord Jesus returns at His 2nd Advent.

**2 Thessalonians 2:7** For the mystery of iniquity doth already work: only he who now letteth will let, until he be taken out of the way. 8 And then shall that Wicked be revealed, whom the Lord shall consume with the spirit of his mouth, and shall destroy with the brightness of his coming: 9 Even him, whose coming is after the working of Satan with all power and signs and lying wonders, 10 And with all deceivableness of unrighteousness in them that perish; because they received not the love of the truth, that they might be saved.

Many in the New Age movement believe that planet Earth is a living being, a goddess named Gaia. They believe that Gaia is communicating with "Ascended Masters of the Hierarchy of the universe." They believe that soon our "space brothers" will raise a human leader from our midst whom they will endow with supernormal powers and wisdom. This man will lead the world to global government and world peace. At some point a world leader will receive power from an alien being known as the "dragon," identified in the Book of Revelation as Satan![93]

---

[93] Lewis, D. & Shreckhise, R., UFO End-Time Delusion, New Leaf, 1991, p 16.

There is much more to this than we have space for here, but the biblical truth presented is that the coming Antichrist will be a man that is not just "possessed of devils," but possessed of Satan himself. That man is the "seed of the serpent." Now how do we know that Jesus is the promised "seed of the woman?" The answer is no problem if you believe what the Bible says about Jesus' birth, that He was born of a virgin. You see, there normally is no such thing as the "seed" of a woman. The man carries the seed. But in the case of Jesus, the only human involved was a woman, since Jesus had no human father. Thus, He is the only one that qualifies in the history of the world to be born of the "seed of the woman." And just in case you were wondering, AI doesn't qualify either since the "seed" of a male is still involved. No. There has only been one virgin birth and that was Jesus Christ.

The reason we discuss all this is so that you can appreciate the subtlety of what Satan is doing. Satan knows that there is a promised Messiah and that he will be the "seed of the woman." That is, he will become a man through human birth. So this plan of intermarrying the fallen angels with the human women not only produces a race of ½ demonic giants, but then the giants intermarry as well, producing offspring that also carry the demonic stamp. Through the course of time, after many generations of intermarrying, the giant aspect may have been diminished, but make no mistake, the offspring are all part of the demonic seed no matter how far removed they are from the original union of the sons of God and daughters of men.

This strategy has the added benefit of contaminating the human gene pool so that a promised Messiah (Gen. 3:15) cannot be born into a demonic line. What a clever plan. Satan can cut off the promised Messiah and at the same time raise up an ever-increasing kingdom of his own. But what is the end game?

*Chapter 10*

# End Game

The world is experiencing more unusual turmoil than ever. The Earth is experiencing as it were- birth pains. But what are these birth pains? What is it that is so near? Do not be fooled. The end game is upon us. We are living in a world that we perceive to be real. Our earth, solar system and our universe are indeed real. Or are they?

The most profound discovery of modern-day physics is that we live in a finite universe. Time has a beginning. It is finite. Infinity is only possible in mathematics. We cannot find infinity anywhere in the universe. Empirically it is not possible to get smaller than Planck's constant. Scientists have now confirmed that our universe is a "shadow of a larger reality!" (Scientific American, June 2005.) The entire volume of our galaxy is filled with diffuse clouds of magnetized plasma—electrically charged ionized particles. 99% of all matter is in the form of plasma![94] We are indeed living in a "digital" environment of what I call the Matrix.

In the movie the Matrix, Neo is trapped in a computer simulation world. He does not know that he is living in a simulation. He only knows that reality. Nevertheless, he seeks a way out of that system; to live beyond what he knows. When he takes the red pill to discover the truth, he follows the rabbit hole to learn that his world is merely a designed computer simulation. Neo's world was death & destruction. There was no meaning to life in his world. As he steps into the next reality called

---

[94] Missler, C., Angels: Angels Vol. 1: The Angelic Realm, Koinonia House, 2012. p.6

Zion, he touches a mirror and enfolds into it. The mirror is liquid and he enters through the mirror into the next world. What was Alice's Adventures in the Looking Glass about? It was about this exactly. She fell into a mirror into another dimension.

In a similar way, Christians will also go through that "mirror" beyond time and space to live independent of this perceived reality. This life is only temporal. As we have discussed - it is indeed the Matrix. The Bible also talks about a mirror. Let's read in the oldest book of the Bible: the book of Job.

### Job 37:18 (KJV)
18 Hast thou with him spread out the sky, which is strong, and as a molten looking glass?

There is a barrier between our world and the next dimension that keeps us separated. But the fallen angels have breached that barrier and have fallen into our time & space into the fourth dimension.[95] It is because UFOs are at least one dimension higher than us; they seem to perform amazing feats that totally defy the law of physics or our known universe.

### Revelation 12:9 (KJV)
9 And the great dragon was cast out, that old serpent, called the Devil, and Satan, which deceiveth the whole world: he was cast out into the earth, and **his angels were cast out with him**.

### Psalm 78:49 (KJV)
49 He cast upon them the fierceness of his anger, wrath, and in dignation, and trouble, **by sending evil angels among them.**

---

[95] The four dimensions are length, width, height, & time.

It is imperative that we understand that we have been thrust into a cosmic battle that involves our very eternity. Whether you like it or not, this is a spiritual battle going on for the souls of mankind. There is an endgame to which this is all heading. It is the ultimate cosmic battle of all time we are so rapidly approaching. It is called the Tribulation, which involves the Battle of Armageddon during the Last Days. These fallen angels are among us again and they will have dominion in the last days over the earth! They are the forerunners of the coming Antichrist!

### Isaiah 14:12-14 (KJV)

12 How art thou fallen from heaven, O Lucifer, son of the morn ing! how art thou cut down to the ground, which didst weaken the nations!

13 For thou hast said in thine heart, I will ascend into heaven, I will exalt my throne above the stars of God: I will sit also upon the mount of the congregation, in the sides of the north:

14 I will ascend above the heights of the clouds; I will be like the most High.

When the Antichrist comes on the scene, the next major event on the timeline is the Tribulation. After Christians have been raptured off of this earth to heaven with the Lord, the world will go through a terrible time called the Tribulation. This event goes by several names.

- Tribulation
- Daniel's 70th Week
- Time of Jacob's Trouble
- The Day of the LORD'S wrath

The book of Daniel tells us that this is a 7-year period of severe judgment. The Antichrist will come on the scene as a peacemaker and broker a covenant between Israel and her enemies, only to break the peace at the mid-point, and attempt to annihilate the nation of Israel.

Revelation tells us that in the last half of the Tribulation, no one will be able to buy or sell without the mark of the beast or the number of his name in their foreheads or hands. Everyone will worship the Antichrist as "god" or be put to death. For those who take his mark and follow him, their eternity will be in the lake of fire. For those who oppose him, he will seek to hunt them down and kill them. The entire book of Revelation is dedicated to giving us details of this most terrible time. We refer to the last half of the Tribulation as the "great tribulation." This is the way the Bible describes it, since its most intense judgments take place during the last 3 ½ years.

Matthew 24 says that there has never been a time so terrible in the history of the world and that there will never again be a time to compare with it. Those who do not receive Jesus Christ as their Savior will miss the Rapture and those who miss the Rapture will likely go into the Tribulation to experience the wrath of God poured out on the earth.

> **Matthew 24:21 (KJV)** For then shall be great tribulation, such as was not since the beginning of the world to this time, no, nor ever shall be.

After the 7 years of Tribulation, the Lord will return with his heavenly army and fight the Battle of Armageddon. This battle will also encompass the 10 nations that confederated with the Antichrist to exterminate Israel during the Tribulation. This is a 10-day event. The Bible says that the bloodshed will be so great that a river of blood the depth of the horse's bridle will run through part of the land. The Lord will crush the enemies of Israel and deliver the believing remnant that has been hidden from the Antichrist during the Tribulation.

The Battle of Armageddon is located in hundreds of verses throughout your Bible. It is a huge event, for it introduces the arrival of the King of Kings - the Lord Jesus Christ. At this battle, the Antichrist and the False Prophet are cast into the lake of fire where they will spend eternity. The Antichrist and the people who join with him shall be destroyed at this battle.

At the Battle of Armageddon:
- The Lord will return visibly
- His heavenly army will return with Him
- He will deliver Israel from her enemies

- He will destroy the 10-nation confederation
- The blood runs to the horse's bridles
- The Antichrist and False Prophet are cast in the lake of fire

The book of Revelation discusses the events leading up to Armageddon. The 7-year period (Tribulation) sees the Antichrist rise to power and create an artificial peace between Israel and her enemies. The Tribulation, or Day of the Lord's Wrath, will officially begin when Israel signs a treaty with the 10 nations around her. This signifies Israel's "Last Days." In order to complete the deception, the man of sin will put down 3 of the 10 nations, give the spoils to Israel and establish a Jewish temple in Jerusalem. Then, the apostate element of Israel will resume their animal sacrifices, in view of their rejection of the sacrifice of Jesus. This is why the book of Hebrews warns against participating in the old sacrificial system; Jesus has already made the only sacrifice that can take away sins!

> **Hebrews 10:1(KJV)**  For the law having a shadow of good things to come, and not the very image of the things, can never with those sacrifices which they offered year by year continually make the comers thereunto perfect. 3 But in those sacrifices there is a remembrance again made of sins every year. 4 For it is not possible that the blood of bulls and of goats should take away sins. 11 And every priest standeth daily ministering and offering oftentimes the same sacrifices, which can never take away sins: 12 But this man, after he had offered one sacrifice for sins for ever, sat down on the right hand of God;

The "man of sin" will be unique. All but the believing remnant (little flock) will be deceived into thinking he is the long awaited Messiah. When this dispensation of grace is over, the final stage of the time schedule for God's program with Israel will resume. When that time comes, if you have not trusted Jesus Christ as your all-sufficient Savior, then you will be left to endure the worst period of suffering in the history of the world.

Here are the main events on the Revelation timeline which will run in this order:

1. Tribulation (Revelation 4-18)

2. 2$^{nd}$ Advent/The Return of Jesus Christ (Revelation 19)

3. Battle of Armageddon (Revelation 19)

4. Satan Bound in Bottomless Pit

5. Millennial Reign of Christ on Earth

6. The Last Great Battle

7. Satan cast into Lake of Fire

8. Great White Throne Judgment

## THE ANTICHRIST

The Antichrist is the final world ruler before Jesus Christ returns to set up His kingdom on this earth. The Bible also calls him the Assyrian.

**Isaiah 10:5 (KJV)** O Assyrian, the rod of mine anger, and the staff in their hand is mine indignation.

Notice the titles: Assyrian and rod of mine anger. He has many other names but there are three descriptive titles in identifying Daniel's "coming prince."

- Man of sin
- Son of Perdition – indwelled by Satan
- Wicked

**2 Thessalonians 2:1 (KJV)**  Now we beseech you, brethren, by the coming of our Lord Jesus Christ, and by our gathering together unto him, 2 That ye be not soon shaken in mind, or be troubled, neither by spirit, nor by word, nor by letter as from us, as that the day of Christ is at hand. 3 Let no man deceive you by any means: for that day shall not come, except there come a falling away first, and that **man of sin** be revealed, the **son of perdition**; 4 Who opposeth and exalteth himself above all that is called God, or that is worshipped; so that he as God sitteth in the temple of God, shewing himself that he is God. 5 Remember ye not, that, when I was yet with you, I told you these things? 6 And now ye know what withholdeth that he might be revealed in his time. 7 For the mystery of iniquity doth already work: only he who now letteth will let, until he be taken out of the way. 8 And then shall that **Wicked** be revealed, whom the Lord shall consume with the spirit of his mouth, and shall destroy with the brightness of his coming:

As a man (the man of sin), he will be the very embodiment of evil. There will be no limit to his wickedness. As the "son of perdition" he will be the "seed of the serpent" spoken of in Genesis 3.

**Genesis 3:15 (KJV)** And I will put enmity between thee and the woman, and between thy seed and her seed; he shall bruise thy head, and thou shalt bruise his heel.

Notice the conflict is between two seeds - the "seed of the woman and the "seed of the serpent." This is where this cosmic battle began. Next, let's examine 6 characteristics of this man we call Antichrist that will help us get a picture of what he will be like.

The word Antichrist implies a double meaning. We know that "anti" means "against" but it can also mean "instead of." The Antichrist fits both of the descriptions at the same time. He is against Christ. At the same time, he seeks to set up a kingdom instead of Christ's. This means that in the Bible we will find many things similar when comparing Jesus Christ and the Antichrist. This is the counterfeiting "instead of" attempt by the Antichrist to convince the world that he is the Messiah.

- Both claim deity
- Both have an army
- Both ride a white horse
- Both have a city that is a bride
- Both are crowned
- Both are accompanied by miracles and signs

We also find that they are opposite to each other. Here the "anti" takes the "against" attitude.

- Son of God vs. Son of Perdition
- The Holy One vs. The Lawless One
- The Mystery of Godliness vs. The Mystery of Iniquity
- Seed of the woman vs. The seed of the serpent
- From Heaven vs. From Bottomless Pit
- The Good Shepherd vs. the Idol Shepherd

The point here is that the world will be deceived by the Antichrist.

**Revelation 13:11 (KJV)** And I beheld another beast coming up out of the earth; and he had two horns like a lamb, and he spake as a dragon. 12 And he exerciseth all the power of the first beast before him, and causeth the earth and them which dwell therein to worship the first beast, whose deadly wound was healed. 13 And he doeth great wonders, so that he maketh fire come down from heaven on the earth in the sight of men, 14 And deceiveth them that dwell on the earth by the means of those miracles which he had power to do in the sight of the beast; saying to them that dwell on the earth, that they should make an image to the beast, which had the wound by a sword, and did live.

**Revelation 12:9 (KJV)** And the great dragon was cast out, that old serpent, called the Devil, and Satan, which deceiveth the whole world: he was cast out into the earth, and his angels were cast out with him.

**2 Thessalonians 2:7 (KJV)** For the mystery of iniquity doth already work: only he who now letteth will let, until he be taken out of the way. 8 And then shall that Wicked be revealed, whom the Lord shall consume with the spirit of his mouth, and shall destroy with the brightness of his coming: 9 Even him, whose coming is after the working of Satan with all power and signs and lying wonders, 10 And with all deceivableness of unrighteousness in them that perish; because they received not the love of the truth, that they might be saved. 11 And for this cause God shall send them strong delusion, that they should believe a lie: 12 That they all might be damned who believed not the truth, but had pleasure in unrighteousness.

The miracles that are performed go a long way to convincing people that the Antichrist is who he says he is, but there is more behind the deception than that. When we see the characteristics of the "beast" then we understand why everyone in general will rush to take the mark. They will believe The Lie.

## 1. The Antichrist will be an intellectual genius

**Daniel 8:23 (KJV)** And in the latter time of their kingdom, when the transgressors are come to the full, a king of fierce countenance, and understanding dark sentences, shall stand up.

**Ezekiel 28:3 (KJV)** Behold, thou art wiser than Daniel; there is no secret that they can hide from thee:

The Ezekiel 28 prophecy is directed at the "prince of Tyrus" who pictures the Antichrist and the "King of Tyrus," which pictures Satan, who indwells the Antichrist. Ezekiel 28:3 is directed at the Antichrist, showing his great wisdom.

## 2. The Antichrist will be a captivating speaker

**Daniel 11:36 (KJV)** And the king shall do according to his will; and he shall exalt himself, and magnify himself above every god, and shall **speak marvellous things against the God of gods**, and shall prosper till the indignation be accomplished: for that that is determined shall be done.

**Revelation 13:5 (KJV)** And there was given unto him a **mouth speaking great things** and blasphemies; and power was given unto him to continue forty and two months. 6 And he opened his mouth in blasphemy against God, to blaspheme his name, and his tabernacle, and them that dwell in heaven.

Here is an amazing point. The Antichrist will represent himself as the true Messiah, but he will not hide the fact that he is against the God of Heaven! He will speak openly against God. The world is moving toward a place where they will readily accept this new message, for it is what they wanted all along. The Antichrist will convince them that it is possible to throw off the constraints of God and live without Him. He will prepare the earth for the 2nd Advent of Jesus Christ and paint the Savior as a "bad alien." He knows where Jesus Christ will come to the earth and he will have the armies of the world gathered there to oppose Christ and His heavenly army.

### Revelation 16:13 (KJV)

13 And I saw three unclean spirits like frogs come out of the mouth of the dragon, and out of the mouth of the beast, and out of the mouth of the false prophet. 14 For they are the spirits of devils, working miracles, which go forth unto the kings of the earth and of the whole world, to gather them to the battle of that great day of God Almighty. 15 Behold, I come as a thief. Blessed is he that watcheth, and keepeth his garments, lest he walk naked, and they see his shame. 16 And he gathered them together into a place called in the Hebrew tongue **Armageddon.**

### Revelation 19:19 (KJV)

19 And I saw the beast, and the kings of the earth, and their armies, gathered together to make war against him that sat on the horse, and against his army.

### 3. The Antichrist will be a powerful politician

### Revelation 17:11 (KJV)

11 And the beast that was, and is not, even he is the eighth, and is of the seven, and goeth into perdition. 12 And the ten horns which thou sawest are ten kings, which have received no kingdom as yet; but receive power as kings one hour with the beast. 13 These have one mind, and shall **give their power and strength unto the beast.**

### Daniel 9:27 (KJV)

27 And he shall **confirm the covenant** with many for one week: and in the midst of the week he shall cause the sacrifice and the oblation to cease, and for the overspreading of abominations he shall make it desolate, even until the consummation, and that determined shall be poured upon the desolate.

### Daniel 8:25 (KJV)

25 And **through his policy** also he shall cause craft to prosper in his hand; and he shall magnify himself in his heart, and by peace

shall destroy many: he shall also stand up against the Prince of princes; but he shall be broken without hand.

## 4. The Antichrist will control the world's economy

**Daniel 11:43 (KJV)**
43 But he shall have power over the treasures of gold and of silver, and over all the precious things of Egypt: and the Libyans and the Ethiopians shall be at his steps.

**Revelation 13:16-17 (KJV)**
16 And he causeth all, both small and great, rich and poor, free and bond, to receive a mark in their right hand, or in their foreheads: 17 And that no man might buy or sell, save he that had the mark, or the name of the beast, or the number of his name.

## 5. The Antichrist will be a military leader

**Revelation 13:4 (KJV)**
4 And they worshipped the dragon which gave power unto the beast: and they worshipped the beast, saying, Who is like unto the beast? who is able to make war with him?

**Revelation 6:2 (KJV)**
2 And I saw, and behold a white horse: and he that sat on him had a bow; and a crown was given unto him: and he went forth conquering, and to conquer.

## 6. The Antichrist will build a 1-world religion around him

**Revelation 13:8 (KJV)**
8 And all that dwell upon the earth shall worship him, whose names are not written in the book of life of the Lamb slain from the foundation of the world.

### Revelation 13:12 (KJV)

12 And he exerciseth all the power of the first beast before him, and causeth the earth and them which dwell therein to worship the first beast, whose deadly wound was healed.

### 2 Thessalonians 2:3 (KJV)

3 Let no man deceive you by any means: for that day shall not come, except there come a falling away first, and that man of sin be revealed, the son of perdition; 4 Who opposeth and exalteth himself above all that is called God, or that is worshipped; so that he as God sitteth in the temple of God, shewing himself that he is God.

### Daniel 11:36 (KJV)

36 And the king shall do according to his will; and he shall exalt himself, and **magnify himself above every god**, and shall speak marvellous things against the God of gods, and shall prosper till the indignation be accomplished: for that that is determined shall be done.

There are 3 principal schools of thought concerning the prophecies that relate to the Antichrist. The first applies these prophecies to people of the past, to men who have been in their graves for many centuries. The second gives these prophecies a present application, finding their fulfillment in the Papacy and the Roman Catholic Church. And the third gives them a future application, and looks for their fulfillment by a man who is yet to be revealed.

It is this third view which the authors hold to. The prophecies concerning the Antichrist have not yet been fulfilled. And they cannot be fulfilled until this present dispensation of grace has run its course. The Holy Spirit now prevents the final outworking of the Mystery of Iniquity and must be removed before the Son of Perdition can be revealed. The Antichrist is not a system of evil or an Antichristian organization. Instead we are speaking of a single, individual person who has yet to appear. Therefore, the Antichrist is yet future as of the writing of this book. This Antichrist's kingdom is outlined for us in Daniel 2 which lists the Gentile world empires in succession.

1. **Head of Gold**- Kingdom of Babylon; more specifically King Nebuchadnezzar (70 years).

2. **Chest & arms of Silver**- the Medo-Persian Empire (49 yrs/7 weeks).

3. **The belly & thighs of Brass**- the Grecian Empire (434 yrs/62 wks). Unlike Nebuchadnezzar and Darius, Alexander is not specifically mentioned by name in the Scripture. However, he is mentioned by another title- the rough goat. This period runs through the days of the Messiah.

> **Daniel 8:20-21 (KJV)** The ram which thou sawest having two horns are the kings of Media and Persia. (You can go back to vv. 3-7 and insert the Medes and Persia for the ram with the two horns) 21 And the **rough goat** is the king of Grecia: and the great horn that is between his eyes is the first king.

4. **The legs of Iron**- Most bible scholars believe this refers to the Roman Empire. However, this nation is not specifically named in the Bible even though it was the next of the Empire nations to rule. Instead, this was the Greco-Roman Empire which eventually split into 2 "legs" of the kingdom under Ptolemy and Seleucus after Alexander the Great.

5. **The feet of Iron & Clay**- This is the 10-nation confederacy of the antichrist kingdom. Although this kingdom is yet future as of 2012, this is what is coming next!

## THE ACTIVITY OF THE ANTICHRIST

There are two names given in 2 Thessalonians that seem to outline the two distinct activities of the Antichrist. One of those being that he is attempting to pass himself off as Jesus Christ. The other being that his is an adversary of Jesus Christ and Israel.

At this present time in the year 2012, the mystery of iniquity is being held back from coming to its completion by the presence of the One New Man (Eph. 2:15), which will result in the revealing of the man - the Antichrist. This present dispensation of grace ends with the Blessed

Hope (Titus 2:13, aka Rapture). The man of sin will not be revealed until after the believers in Jesus Christ have been removed.

The book of Daniel outlines the events that lead up to the Antichrist's appearance, before Daniel's 70th Week begins. We know this since he will be the one who confirms the covenant with Israel. Although the Antichrist will start out small from a governmental standpoint, he will quickly rise to be a world power. In 1957, Henry Spaak, Belgium's most prominent politician declared:

"We do not want another committee: we have too many already. What is needed is a man of sufficient stature to hold the allegiance of all people and to lift us out of the economic morass into which we are sinking. Send us such a man and, be he god or devil, we will receive him."[96]

He will make an unusual appearance to the world (perhaps in a UFO) when he ascends out of the Bottomless Pit, which we will not discuss here. Since the Antichrist is going to pass himself off as the Messiah to the Jewish people, it would make sense for him to make a "grand entry" at Jerusalem like Christ. Once he is in Jerusalem, he will pose as Christ to Israel, as the "Prince of Peace." But then the "Red Horse" of the Apocalypse makes his entrance and peace is taken from the earth.

When the Antichrist comes to power, there will be 10 horns who have the "power" of kings already in place. He will overthrow 3 of these and the remaining 7 will make obeisance to the Antichrist.

**Revelation 17:12 (KJV)** And the ten horns which thou sawest are ten kings, which have received no kingdom as yet; but receive power as kings one hour with the beast.

**Daniel 7:24 (KJV)** And the ten horns out of this kingdom are ten kings that shall arise: and another shall rise after them; and he shall be diverse from the first, and he shall subdue three kings.

---

[96] Dr. David A. Lewis, Prophecy 2000, New Leaf Press, p 61.

These 10 horns are pictured by the 10 toes (of iron and clay) in Daniel 2. These 10 rise out of the 4th kingdom of Daniel's image (Zech. 6:1). These 10 have been the subject of Scripture from the beginning. References include: Genesis 15 and Psalm 83.

## ALIEN ABDUCTIONS

A very disturbing characteristic of the current UFO reports are the continuing cases involving "abductions" of people and the strange behavior associated with them. It is estimated that only 3-5% of the population has reported being involved in abductions. What is the common denominator? Implantation and harvesting of human fetuses appear to be the primary focus. Could this be a form of repetition of the strange events of Genesis 6?

Having an interest in the UFO phenomena, I had done some research into discovering what was really going on. After all, UFO sightings and close encounters were being documented around the world. Again, while most of these are not genuine, some things seemed worth investigation. It was about this same time that I met a man named Charlie Hickson who was from Pascagoula, Mississippi.

Charlie spoke with me about an encounter he had with a UFO and its occupants just a few years back. He recounted how he and a friend of his had gone fishing. While they were fishing, through some means unknown to Charlie, he and his friend were paralyzed; that is, they could not move. But they could see. Both men watched as they were taken aboard a craft of some kind and some kinds of experiments were done on them. The details of this are not important, but here is what is. At some point they lost conscious perception of what was happening. When they awakened back at their fishing spot, they both recalled the same event. The difference was that Charlie's friend suffered some kind of mental breakdown over the incident that, I was given to understand, he never fully recovered from. Charlie did not seem to me to be some kind of publicity hound or to be a man after notoriety.

I have no personal knowledge as to the extent to which Charlie's friend was affected and I have left his name out of this work on purpose.

But I do believe that something happened to Charlie and I also believe that something to be the work of Satan as he prepares the world for a coming deception in which his man, the Antichrist, will be viewed as a god.

"The idea that men, women, and children can be taken against their wills, from their homes, cars, and school yards by strange humanoid beings, lifted onto space craft, and subjected to intrusive and threatening procedures is so terrifying and yet so shattering to our notions of what is possible in our universe, that the actuality of the phenomena has been largely rejected out of hand or bizarrely distorted in most media accounts...this is all together understandable, given the disturbing nature of UFO abductions and our prevailing notions of reality. The fact remains, however, that for 30 years, and possibly longer, thousands of individuals who seem to be sincere and of sound mind, and who are seeking no personal benefit from their stories, have been providing to those who will listen consistent reports of precisely such events."— John Mack, M.D.

Remember after Genesis 6 we see a repeat of the giants post-flood. Genesis 6:4 "...also after that..." These are the Rephaim, Emim, Horim, Zamsummim in Gen 14, 15; Arba, Anak & his 7 sons (Anakim), encountered in Canaan (Numbers 13:33); Og, King of Bashan (Deut 3:11; Josh 12); Goliath and his 4 brothers.

So we know that the Nephilim came back after the flood. Not because any survived Noah's Deluge - they were ALL wiped out! But it was the return of the Nephilim that caused them to repopulate. Proponents such as Eric von Daniken and Stichin believe that it is the Annunnaki (the sons of Anak - "those from the heavens came") who are the ETs and seeded the human race with their genetics by means of evolution. What a twist! It is completely contradictory from the Genesis account that we are a special creation from God. What you may not know is that those Annunnaki are actually the Nephilim of Genesis 6! They are not extraterrestrials from another planet.

Of all the things that were happening before the flood, the intermarrying of "sons of God" with "daughters of men" was one of the most significant. Could it be that the Nephilim will make their appearance again in the Tribulation?

# THE RETURN OF THE NEPHILIM

Let's see what's so unusual about these ten kings who have "power" with the beast.

> **Daniel 2:42-43 (KJV)**
> [42] And *as* the toes of the feet *were* part of iron, and part of clay, *so* the kingdom shall be partly strong, and partly broken.
> [43] And whereas thou sawest iron mixed with miry clay, **they shall mingle themselves with the seed of men**: but they shall not cleave one to another, even as iron is not mixed with clay.

So what is this "miry clay?" Miry clay is clay made from mire & dust. Daniel says that they will mingle themselves **with the seed of men; but they shall not cleave to each other**". But who are "they?" They are the Fallen Angels! And the 10 kings are the return of the Nephilim in Revelation! This is the Alien Agenda: to usher in the kingdom of the Antichrist and to prepare for the coming cosmic battle! The forces of evil are planning for Armageddon, and they are breeding a hybrid species for the battle. They did it back in the Old Testament days (the giants) to corrupt mankind's genes and they are doing it again! This is a repeat of the Days of Noah! It is the return of the Nephilim.

> **Matthew 24:37 (KJV)**
> [37] But as the days of Noe *were*, so shall also the coming of the Son of man be.

The Nephilim are returning! And they will show up at the Battle of Armageddon. I understand for many of you this is difficult to accept. Not only is this exactly what the Bible tells us what happened in the past, it also tells us that it will happen again in the Tribulation (which will follow the Rapture event). The Genesis 6 event is going to be happening all over again in the future!

Daniel is prophesying about the last days. Here we read that the activity of Genesis 6 would be repeated in the last days and the Nephilim will return during this time. They will come down in the "likeness of men" and describe themselves as from the planet Nibiru or some other planet according to modern day New Agers.

The book of Jude confirms Daniels prophecy:

**Jude 1:6-7 (KJV)**
[6] And the *angels* **which kept not their first estate, <u>but left their own habitation</u>,** he hath reserved in everlasting chains under darkness unto the judgment of the great day.
[7] Even as Sodom and Gomorrha, and the cities about them in like manner, giving themselves over to fornication, and **<u>going after strange flesh</u>,** are set forth for an example, suffering the vengeance of eternal fire.

> This is a repeat of the "days of Noah"- the return of the Nephilim!

The final Gentile world Empire will be as "iron mixed with miry clay." But just as verse 43 states in Daniel 2, "they shall not cleave one to another, even as iron is not mixed with clay." This is the "10 toes" of Daniel. It will be the time of the Antichrist. This is a repeat of the "days of Noah"- the return of the Nephilim! The Coming World Leader will be characterized by the working of the supernatural, with lying signs and wonders! The world is getting ready for a great deception, just as was happening back in the days of Noah. That deception will include the fact that people will not hear the Bible. They are carried away with a "feel-good" religion that has no content other than to make them feel good about themselves. For those of you who really dig into the Bible, you can find those "mingled people" over in Jeremiah 25.

The modern speculation has these 10 nations as a European Union. But they are not from the Revived Roman Empire. They are first listed for you in the book of Genesis when God makes His covenant with Abram concerning the land grant He will give to the nation of Israel; the nation that will come from Abraham. In Satan's contention over the land of Israel, these 10 have always been players from the very beginning. Notice that on the heels of lining out the boundaries of the land that God is promising to Abraham's seed, he lists the 10 "nations" that are already present in that land grant. They are all listed in vv. 20-21. Go ahead, count them.

> **Genesis 15:18 (KJV)**  In the same day the LORD made a covenant with Abram, saying, Unto thy seed have I given this land, from the river of Egypt unto the great river, the river Euphrates: [19] **The Kenites, and the Kenizzites, and the Kadmonites,** [20] **And the Hittites, and the Perizzites, and the Rephaims,** [21] **And the Amorites, and the Canaanites, and the Girgashites, and the Jebusites.**

Almost every student of prophecy is aware of the "ten kings" of Revelation 17. These will occupy the same land areas as the ten in Genesis 15. The names may change over the years, but the area remains the same. When the time of the end comes and the Antichrist is ruling, the 10 kings that occupy the same land area of the ten nations of Genesis 15 will confederate with him.

> **Revelation 17:11 (KJV)** And the beast that was, and is not, even he is the eighth, and is of the seven, and goeth into perdition. [12] And the ten horns which thou sawest are ten kings, which have received no kingdom as yet; but receive power as kings one hour with the beast. [13] These have one mind, and shall give their power and strength unto the beast.

When you look at the entire land grant promised by God to Israel, you will see that other nations are always present on parts of the land grant. They are Satan's ever-present tools against the nation. Even when God expels the people out of their land under the hand of Nebuchadnezzar, what happens to Israel happens to these other "nations?" They nations of Genesis 15 are the same nations from which will rise the 10 kings who will give their power to the beast. As you read Jeremiah's pronouncement against Israel, take a look at who is swept up by the Babylonians. Not just Israel, but also "all these nations round about." What are those nations? They are the ones we have seen from the beginning, but now we are made to see that they are not European nations, for they are "round about" Israel!

**Jeremiah 25:9 (KJV)** Behold, I will send and take all the families of the north, saith the LORD, and Nebuchadrezzar the king of Babylon, my servant, and will bring them against this land, and against the inhabitants thereof, and against all these nations round about, and will utterly destroy them, and make them an astonishment, and an hissing, and perpetual desolations.

These are the nations that confederate with the Antichrist in the last days. And that is the perfect word for that is the very word the Bible uses to describe their actions. These are Satan's minions, Satan's nations. They hate Israel and will help the Antichrist in his extermination policy against Israel.

**Psalms 83:1 (KJV)** <<A Song or Psalm of Asaph.>> Keep not thou silence, O God: hold not thy peace, and be not still, O God. [2] For, lo, thine enemies make a tumult: and they that hate thee have lifted up the head. [3] They have taken crafty counsel against thy people, and consulted against thy hidden ones. [4] They have said, Come, and let us cut them off from *being* a nation; that the name of Israel may be no more in remembrance. [5] For they have consulted together with one consent: **they are confederate against thee:** [6] **The tabernacles of Edom, and the Ishmaelites; of Moab, and the Hagarenes;** [7] **Gebal, and Ammon, and Amalek; the Philistines with the inhabitants of Tyre;** [8] **Assur also is joined with them:** they have holpen the children of Lot. Selah.

Even though their names have changed throughout history, they are "round about Israel" and will seek to destroy her in the Last Days. These are those 10 nations (along with the children of Lot) that will be involved with the Antichrist in the Tribulation, when the great deception reaches its zenith. These are the same as the "ten horns" of Daniel 7.

**Daniel 7:24 (KJV)** And the ten horns out of this kingdom are ten kings that shall arise: and another shall rise after them; and he shall be diverse from the first, and he shall subdue three kings.

It is not our intent to produce an entire study on this issue, only to educate you as to how things will shape up in the end times. I would heartily recommend, for anyone who is truly interested in getting a good, solid biblical foundation in these issues, to either get Millennium Bible Institute's study on Revelation and Daniel (available on DVD) or at least get David Winston Busch's book titled, *The Assyrian*. Either of these will

give you an education on how the nations line up in the last days.

The Antichrist, identified as the Assyrian & the king of the North, brings a false peace and false security to Israel. He assumes the kingdom through flatteries and the appearance of peace. He confirms a covenant with "many;" the 10 nations and Israel, for these are the major players in the conflict over the land of Israel. We saw these 10 first named in Genesis 15. The Antichrist will bring that long awaited peace to Israel and the Middle East in the beginning; but it is a false peace. We refer to it as a "false peace" because the intent of the Antichrist is to lure the Jews into a false sense of security. Then in the "midst of the week" or 3 & 1/2 years later, we see the Antichrist turn on the Jews and seek to exterminate them. Jesus warned them in Matthew that this would take place when they saw the abomination of desolation, and they should then flee to the mountains.

> **2 Thessalonians 2:4 (KJV)** Who opposeth and exalteth himself above all that is called God, or that is worshipped; so that he as God sitteth in the temple of God, shewing himself that he is God.

The last half of Daniel's 70th Week sees the terrible judgments poured out on the earth as the Beast seeks to lure the Jewish remnant out of hiding. The Tribulation ends at a prescribed time, with the last half being designated "the Great Tribulation" which is 1260 days in length. At that point the sun, moon and stars go dark and the "hidden ones" recognize the sign of their Messiah's Advent. The Advent of Jesus Christ does not happen immediately when the heavens go dark. There is a 30-day period between the actual end of the Tribulation and the Advent itself. It is during this 30-day period that things begin to fall apart for the Antichrist. The 10 kings that joined with the Antichrist will now turn on him, as the Scriptures say that those 10 kings only give their power to the Antichrist for a prescribed period of time.

It is the Armageddon Campaign that will see the Lord taking possession again of all the earth. He will have gathered the armies of the nations together and confederate with the Antichrist in one place to do battle with them. These armies will be completely destroyed in this fight and the Lord will set up his Kingdom on Earth and rule from Jerusalem for 1,000 years! This is called the Millennial Reign.

| JESUS CHRIST | ANTICHRIST |
|---|---|
| He is King of Kings – Rev. 19 | He is king over children of pride – Job 41 |
| He is the "angel of God" – Gal. 4:14 | He appears as an "angel of light" – 2 Cor. 11 |
| He is the "light of the world." – John 8:12 | He appears as "angel of light" – 2 Cor. 11 |
| He is "God…manifest in the flesh – I Tim. 3 | He is "god of this world" – 2 Cor. 4:4 |
| He has a bride which is a city – Rev. 21:9 | He has a bride which is a city – Rev. 17 |
| He cites Scripture – Luke 4 | He cites Scripture – Luke 4 |
| He preaches 42 months – Luke 3, John 2,5,6 | He preaches 42 months – Rev. 13:5 |
| Christ means "anointed" – Acts 4:26, Ps. 2:2 | Satan is "anointed" as a "Christ" – Ez. 28 |
| He is "prince of peace" – Isa. 9:6 | He is "prince of this world" – John 14:30 |
| He is "lion of tribe of Judah" – Rev. 5:5 | He is a "roaring lion" – I Peter 5:8 |
| Performs miracles, signs and wonders – Matthew 9:32, Mark 6:2 | Performs miracles, signs and wonders –Matt. 24:2; 2 Thess. 2:9 |
| Is God – John 1:1-2; 10:35 | He claims to be God – 2 Thess. 2:4 |
| Followers sealed in the Tribulation – Rev. 7:4; 14:1 | Followers sealed in forehead or hand in Tribulation – Rev. 13:16-18 |
| Rides a white horse – Rev. 19:11 | Rides a white horse – Rev. 6:2 |
| Dies and resurrects – I Cor. 15:3-4 | Dies and resurrects – Rev.13:3, 12 |
| Has a Second Coming – Rev. 19 | Has a Second Coming – Rev. 17:8, 11 |
| Part of the holy trinity: Father, Son and Holy Ghost | Part of unholy trinity: Satan, Antichrist and false prophet |

# Summary

There is an old saying that coming events cast their shadows. What is the purpose behind all this? Is there a pattern of evil - a pattern than can only be evil because of the sinister forces involved? Time will tell. In the meantime, let us be on guard, especially in the spiritual realm. UFO sightings can sometimes be attributed to hoaxes and hallucinations, but more often they are very real in the fullest sense. At times it becomes clear that spiritual forces are involved.[97] As Paul warned Timothy, people today are vulnerable to "buy in" to signs and wonders without considering their source. We also learned of the activities of the Antichrist with lying signs and wonders. The UFO phenomena is certainly associated with and is casting its shadow of what is to come.

**UFOs are either...**
→   real or not real

→   scientific or supernatural

→   natural or hoax

→   causes or hallucinations

→   human intelligence or benevolent angels

→   extraterrestrial intelligence or malevolent (demonic)

UFOs may be a set up for the unsaved in the world to receive the coming Antichrist, his military during the tribulation and the raising up of

---

[97] Wilson, C. UFO's & Their Mission Impossible, Signet, 1974, pg. 97

a Nephilim army to fight against Jesus Christ. There is a coming delusion and after the Rapture, the deception will engulf many.

**Matthew 24:4 (KJV)**
[4] And Jesus answered and said unto them, Take heed that no man **deceive** you.

**Matthew 24:24 (KJV)**
[24] For there shall arise false Christs, and false prophets, and shall shew great signs and wonders; insomuch that, if *it were* possible, they **shall deceive** the very elect.

> Suppression is not a disbelief of the truth but a denial of it.

## SUPPRESSION OF THE TRUTH

Truth is the direct opposite of falsehood and is the first to get repressed in any lie. Just as we defined sin, we need to define truth. Pilot asked Jesus, "What is truth"? Truth is defined as a verified or indisputable fact, proposition, principle, or the like: mathematical truths. More specifically, it is when the word and the deed become one. Jesus Christ is The Truth. But there will be some who deny him. What a tragedy for you to learn what's in this book regarding what the Bible has to say about evolution and the UFO phenomena and never come to the knowledge of the truth!

**2 Timothy 3:1-8 (KJV)**
[1] This know also, that in the last days perilous times shall come.
[2] For men shall be lovers of their own selves, covetous, boasters, proud, blasphemers, disobedient to parents, unthankful, unholy,
[3] Without natural affection, trucebreakers, false accusers, incontinent, fierce, despisers of those that are good,
[4] Traitors, heady, highminded, lovers of pleasures more than lovers of God;

[5] Having a form of godliness, but denying the power thereof: from such turn away.

[6] For of this sort are they which creep into houses, and lead captive silly women laden with sins, led away with divers lusts,

[7] ***Ever learning, and never able to come to the knowledge of the truth.***

[8] Now as Jannes and Jambres withstood Moses, so do these also resist the truth: men of corrupt minds, reprobate concerning the faith.

### 2 Timothy 4:3-4 (KJV)

[3] For the time will come when they will not endure sound doctrine; but after their own lusts shall they heap to themselves teachers, having itching ears;

[4] And **they shall turn away** *their* **ears from the truth, and shall be turned unto fables**.

### Romans 1:25 (KJV)

[25] **Who changed the truth of God into a lie**, and worshipped and served the creature more than the Creator, who is blessed for ever. Amen.

Suppression leads to oppression. To suppress something is to resist it consciously. Suppression is not a disbelief of the truth but a denial of it. There is a world of difference between ignorance of the truth and a denial of it. One would expect the world to "suppress the truth." But the Bible tells us that the truth sets us free. The pursuit of truth should be our highest priority. Jesus spoke to his little flock about truth.

### John 14:4-6 (KJV)

[4] And whither I go ye know, and the way ye know.

[5] Thomas saith unto him, Lord, we know not whither thou goest; and how can we know the way?

[6] Jesus saith unto him, **I am the way, the truth, and the life**: no man cometh unto the Father, but by me.

**John 8:32 (KJV)**
³² And ye shall know the truth, and the truth shall make you free.

The existence of God and the laws of physics, mathematics, logic etc. do not have to be defended. They are proven and fixed in place. They are unchangeable. That's why we call them a LAW. Thomas Jefferson, in his writing of the Declaration, paraphrased the book of Romans by calling them "self-evident" truths. Something that is self-evident, (obvious) needs no trial to determine its veracity. The Holy Scriptures tell us that truth is obvious. We just have to read the Bible.

In fact, those who deny truth are engaging in self-deception. Because the Creator has made the truth "obvious" to everyone, we will never be able to stand before Him and plead *"I didn't know."* By allowing these lies to go unchallenged, Christians permit the truth of God to become a lie. America is upside down. Right is wrong and wrong is right. Lies become true and truth becomes lies. However, lies can only become the new truth if they go unchallenged. Lies rule the day because the truth has been sacrificed.

You see, there is a spiritual problem in America; not a political one. I hear a lot of folks talking about the need to "return" to the Constitution; "rebuild" the nation; "recover" economically, "reclaim" our government; and "restore" the economy. The problem in America is not that the sinners are acting according to their nature, but that Christians are not acting like theirs. Instead of joining in the suppression of Truth it is time for Christians to stand up and defend it.

*We must demand the Truth, expect the Truth, speak the Truth, share the Truth and live the Truth!*

As Christians, we are not constantly searching these matters out because we do not have the answer; we know the truth. It is in the person of Jesus Christ as found in the pages of Scripture. We have been set free from "the law of sin and death" and are made alive in Christ. I like to equate this with the movie The Matrix, as this is a good correlation between living in a world of sin and death, and being reborn (spiritually saved) into newness of life. The Matrix (sin) no longer has power over us. We have been taken out of this matrix by the Gospel of the grace of God. So how do Christians answer these four questions?

Who am I? From the beginning, man was created to be a godly (made in God's likeness) creature.

Where did I come from? Origin with created design; I came from the special creation of God.

What is my purpose here? To labor with God in what He is doing, and through intimacy of fellowship with Him in the Father/son relationship, bring Him glory by putting on display His manifold wisdom.

Where am I going? I am going to the heavenly places, where my future will consist of engaging in my heavenly Father's business as a son who has been equipped to do so.

It is evident that there is an affront on Christianity, attacking its very foundation.[98] If ETs could be verified outside our planet, Carl Sagan said it would be our "turning point in human history."[99] Distinguished Rice University historian of astronomy, Albert van Helden stated, "If it turns out to be true, it would be a compelling demonstration that life on Earth is not that unique."[100] The scenario theorized by the ancient astronaut advocates is based on deductive reasoning & conclusions drawn from postulations that require just as much faith as believing in Hebrews 11:3 which says, "By faith we understand that the worlds were framed by the word of God, so that the things which are seen were not made of things which are visible." The world is looking for an answer other than the supernatural, omnipotent, omniscient, and omnipresent Creator God of the Bible. Despite this fact, people continue to ask the

---

[98] See the book, "The Foundation for Faith" at
http://www.lulu.com/spotlight/ajudkins
[99] Monmaney, Terence. "Just how earth-shaking is life-on-Mars discovery? *Los Angeles Times* report, *Denver Post*, 2 September 1996, 2A.
[100] Ibid

four great questions of life but never come to the knowledge of the truth. The Bible has already given us these answers and has revealed the Truth in the person of Jesus Christ.

Regrettably, mankind continues to look for answers outside the truth of Jesus Christ. They look in our planet, up in the heavens with its galaxies, and solar systems and ask, "Is the cosmos seeded with other life?" "What if the Panspermia Theory is true?" "What if life originated outside our galaxy?" "What if we find water on another planet?" However, water is not the only quality required for life. "What if we were genetically altered?" "What if we are actually aliens evolved over millions of years of time"? What if, what if, what if.... As my history teacher used to sarcastically say- it's the big "what if" game! Now let me pose some questions for you. What if the theory of evolution is wrong? What if the ancient astronaut theory is wrong? What if the Bible is right after all? What if God exists?

"And Jesus Christ has promised to return, another aspect which von Daniken seizes on as being a constant theme of the gods-[ancient] astronauts - of old. But there is a difference, not the least being the descriptions and clues given as to the events to take place preceding that return."- Clifford Wilson[101]

As you consider the theories of life's origins, the UFO phenomena, and what you have now learned in this book, you must decide if you will accept what God's word says. The Bible is more than a metaphysical interpretation. It is supernatural in origin and written by inspiration of God. It is about the redemption of mankind from a fallen sinful nature!

## LET'S LOOK TO SEE WHERE ALL THIS IS TAKING US

✓ UFOs are real

✓ UFO flaps have been every 4 years, 8 months. A "flap" is a sharp increase in the number of sightings.

---

[101] Wilson, Clifford, Crash Go The Chariots, Lancer Books, 1972, p. 74

✓ Fallen Angels do not require a body to live in

✓ They do not need a vehicle to travel in

✓ They are the size and appearance of men

✓ Devils or demons are the spirits of Nephilim who have died

✓ The occupants of UFOs have some degree of connection to the demonic

Why would demons want to impersonate beings from another world? Let's ask another question. Why would demons want to impersonate the dead? The answer to both is the same; deception.

## THINK ABOUT THE FOLLOWING FACTS

→ One of the dominant cultural influences of UFOs is to undermine faith in the Bible

→ UFO phenomena supports the myth of evolution

→ UFO phenomena supports the idea that man can be perfect apart from God; ignores or denies the redemption of Christ on the cross.

→ UFO phenomena denigrate the Bible since it is an "earthbound" book for an inferior civilization

→ They offer no peace of mind & at times people have detected "mental voices"

→ They are associated with extremely foul odors, aversion to strong light, a shadowy or translucent figure, & a sudden decrease in temperature

## MAIN CHARACTERISTICS OF UFOs

✓ UFOs have an affinity for electricity and power stations

✓ UFOs are often sighted around bodies of water and have been witnessed entering and exiting the ocean

✓ UFOs dramatically manipulate matter and energy

✓ UFOs may be in the form of plasma energy

✓ UFOs range in size from a few feet to miles in diameter-

✓ UFOs contain intra-terrestrial visitors, from inside the earth

✓ the occupants of UFOs are described as small; 3-5 feet tall

✓ UFOs defy physics in their flight manner

✓ UFOs cause no sonic boom when accelerating past the sound barrier

✓ UFOs can become visible and invisible at will

✓ UFOs are connected with the new age movement

✓ UFOs are connected with the occult

✓ UFOs/ETs/Hybrids are subject to the name of Jesus

✓ The UFO literature proclaims the one-day meeting of this life in UFOs is the most important day in the history of mankind.

✓ UFOs are conditioning the world where the entrance of one who will claim to be from outside this world.

✓ The Antichrist will deceive the world into thinking he is God.

# WHAT TO DO IF YOU SEE A UFO

-Try and get another or as many additional witnesses as possible

-If you have a camera or cell phone with a camera, take as many pictures as possible. Get as much background or foreground detail as possible. Immediately after your sighting, make complete notes of everything you saw, all the details you can remember. Write down the appearance, color, motion and size of the UFO. Write down what you were thinking and feeling as you saw it. Write down the names and addresses of the other witnesses. If the UFO touched the ground, do what you can to protect the area-but do not disturb the area. Take photos of the area to document it. Report your sighting: call the center for UFO studies at 773-271-3611, 24 hours a day. If no one is at the office, leave a message and an investigator will contact you soon.

# IF YOU HAVE AN ENCOUNTER WITH AN ALIEN OR UFO [102]

**1.** Reject any invitations, deny any requests, and flee any involvement. (Romans 13:12; Ephesians 5:11)

**2.** Take command of your mind & actions. Do not be fooled or impressed. Remember who you are in Jesus Christ and that Satan's policy of evil is always looking for a way to deceive you. (Col 1:13).

---

[102] Missler, C. Angels Vol. 2, The Invisible War, Koinonia House, 2012, pp. 33-34

**1 Corinthians 14:33 (KJV)**
[33] For **God is not *the author* of confusion,** but of peace, as in all churches of the saints.

**3.** Seek counsel from someone who clearly has a Biblical background

**4.** Do not open yourself up to the encounter

**2 Timothy 1:7 (KJV)**
[7] For God hath not given us the spirit of fear; but of power, and of love, and of a sound mind.

**5.** It is a spiritual war. You are a target. The enemy's primary weapon is deception and deceit. Your primary weapon is the word of God. Your battle armor is listed in Ephesians 6:10–18. You should know these seven essential elements.

**Ephesians 6:11-17 (KJV)**
[11] Put on the whole armour of God, that ye may be able to stand against the wiles of the devil.
[12] For we wrestle not against flesh and blood, but against principalities, against powers, against the rulers of the darkness of this world, against spiritual wickedness in high *places*.
[13] Wherefore take unto you the whole armour of God, that ye may be able to withstand in the evil day, and having done all, to stand.
[14] Stand therefore, having your loins girt about with truth, and having on the breastplate of righteousness;
[15] And your feet shod with the preparation of the gospel of peace;
[16] Above all, taking the shield of faith, wherewith ye shall be able to quench all the fiery darts of the wicked.
[17] And take the helmet of salvation, and the sword of the Spirit, which is the word of God:

If you are found to be without Jesus Christ when the Rapture takes place, you will be left behind. Don't be left behind! It's not too late. You can be saved today. Just read about what it will be like if you are left behind.

### Luke 21:25-28 (KJV)

<sup></sup>25 And there shall be signs in the sun, and in the moon, and in the stars; and upon the earth distress of nations, with perplexity; the sea and the waves roaring;

26 **Men's hearts failing them for fear, and for looking after those things which are coming on the earth**: for the powers of heaven shall be shaken.

27 And then shall they see the Son of man coming in a cloud with power and great glory.

28 And when these things begin to come to pass, then look up, and lift up your heads; for your redemption draweth nigh.

### Matthew 24:21-24 (KJV)

21 For then shall be great tribulation, such as was not since the beginning of the world to this time, no, nor ever shall be.

22 And except those days should be shortened, there should no flesh be saved: but for the elect's sake those days shall be shortened.

23 Then if any man shall say unto you, Lo, here *is* Christ, or there; believe *it* not.

24 **For there shall arise false Christs, and false prophets, and shall shew great signs and wonders; insomuch that, if *it* were possible, they shall deceive the very elect.**

## WHAT TO DO TO AVOID THE DECEPTION

-Be saved! Read John 3:16. Ask Jesus into your heart. This is the single most important thing you can do so that you're not left behind!

God sent His Son into the world so that you could be reconciled to God and He reconciled you so that He could utilize you in His plan and purpose. What a privilege!

**2 Corinthians 5:19 (KJV)** To wit, that God was in Christ, reconciling the world unto himself, not imputing their trespasses unto them; and hath committed unto us the word of reconciliation.

-Learn the Bible

-Rightly divide the Word of God

-Use the correct version (the Authorized King James Version)

-Learn correct doctrine for today (the books of Romans - Philemon are written specifically for you and about you)

-Understand how the age will end (in apostasy, and then the Rapture)

-Learn godly wisdom vs. the wisdom of men

-Get in with a group of Bible believers

## WHAT TO DO IF YOU MISS THE RAPTURE

-Don't take the mark of the beast!

-Believe the preaching of the 144,000 in the first half of the Tribulation and the two witnesses (Moses and Elijah) in the second half of the Tribulation

-Believe the Everlasting Gospel if you are a Gentile

-Believe the Gospel of the Kingdom if you are a Jew

-Do everything you can to help the believing remnant of Israel, even at the peril of your own life; your eternity rests on it (Matthew 25:31-45)

-Realize things are different. You will no longer be in a dispensation of grace, but you will be a Gentile in Israel's program.

The real issue is: "Do you know Jesus Christ as your Savior?" Will you leave in the rapture before the tribulation? Are you ready to meet God? Do you know for sure where you will spend eternity?

You can be sure of your eternity if you will put your faith in Jesus Christ. He died on the cross to pay for the sins of the world. The Bible says that "whosoever shall call upon the name of the Lord shall be saved." You can call on him to save you right now. If you are uncertain of what to say, remember that God is not as concerned with the words you use as the attitude of your heart. Trust Him, and Him alone for all that you need to be saved from the debt and penalty of your sin. Commit yourself to him as a demonstration of gratitude for God's gift of salvation; make a decision to live for Jesus every day. This is the greatest decision you will ever make in your entire life! Don't wait till you find yourself a part of the Alien Agenda and the coming Delusion! Find the Truth for yourself in the person of Jesus Christ. He is waiting for you to trust in Him!

> The real issue is:
>
> "Are you born again?"

# About the Authors

## A.S.Judkins

Dr. Judkins is an author, archaeologist and speaker having a passion for teaching Apologetics. He is credited with mapping the longest contiguous dinosaur trackway in the Western Hemisphere near Glen Rose, Texas in the year 2000. That same year, Dr. Judkins discovered a new theropod dinosaur trail in the Paluxy River named in his honor-"The Judkins Trail." He has participated in numerous excavations throughout the U.S. and Israel including the Pool of Siloam in Jerusalem in 2004. Dr. Judkins has been featured on TBN's "Creation in the 21st Century" with Dr. Carl Baugh and the History Channel as well as multiple radio broadcasts. He hosts his own internet show called "Man vs. Archaeology" exposing forbidden archaeology & the mysteries of the past. His Ph.D. is in Biblical Archaeology from Bible Believers Christian College in Los Angeles, CA. To contact A.S. Judkins for interviews or speaking engagements, email manvsarchaeology@gmail.com.

You can follow Dr. Judkins via Twitter: @JudkinsA,
www.facebook.com/ManvsArchaeology
www.manvsarchaeology.wordpress.com
www.youtube.com/XIndianaJones1
www.aaronjudkins.com

Previous books by A.S. Judkins: "The Foundation for Faith" "Academic Freedom: Exposing Evolution" & "Evolution & Human Fossil Footprints".

## Michael McDaniel

Dr. McDaniel is the co-founder and director of the Millennium Bible Institute and pastor of Bible Fellowship church in Monahans, TX. He is a featured lecturer in the Schools of Biblical Studies, Eschatology, and Theological Studies at MBI campuses in Glen Rose, TX and Monahans, TX. He received his Masters degree in Theology and doctorate in Biblical Studies from Pacific International University of St. Louis, Missouri. Dr. McDaniel currently resides in Imperial, TX with his wife, Billie.

The Millennium Bible Institute operates under the umbrella of Bible Fellowship church, which is an independent, non-denominational, self-governing local assembly of Bible believers not affiliated with any organization or denomination. MBI currently carries out live classroom instruction in Glen Rose, Texas and Monahans, Texas. Correspondence instruction is provided by means of printed materials, audio CD, MP3 and DVD formats. You can become a correspondence student by contacting them at www.graceage.org or email at mbipresident@windstream.net or barebonesproduction@gmail.com. Check out Mike's blog at www.mikesbarebones.com.

## Millennium Bible Institute

**PO BOX 305 – Imperial, TX 79743**

**888-605-3202 or 432-242-6000**

MILLENNIUM BIBLE INSTITUTE

# SELECTED BIBLIOGRAPHY

Alnor, W. UFO's in the New Age, Baker Books, 1992

Bates, G. Alien Intrusion, Master Books, 2004

Baugh, C. Evolution Against All Odds, Hearthstone, 1999

Chittick, Don, The Puzzle of Ancient Man, Creation Compass, 2nd Ed. 1998

DeHaan, M.R., The Days of Noah, Zondervan Publishing House, Grand Rapids MI, 1963.

Eberhart, George M., UFOs and the Extraterrestrial Contact Movement: A Bibliography, 2 vols., Scarecrow Press, London 1986.

Eastman, Mark, As the Days of Noah Were (audio publication), Genesis Outreach, Murrietta CA, 1996.

Fleming, John, The Fallen Angels and the Heroes of Mythology, Hodges, Foster, and Figgis, Dublin, 1879.

Hynek, J. Allen, The UFO Report, Dell Publishing Co., NY, 1977.

Judkins, A., Academic Freedom: Exposing Evolution, Maverick Publishing, 2007

Judkins, A., Evolution & Human Fossil Footprints, Bible Belt Publishing,, 2009

Larson, Bob, UFO's & the Alien Agenda, Thomas Nelson Publishers, 1997

Lewis, D. & Shreckhise, R., UFO End-Time Delusion, New Leaf, 1991

McDaniel, Michael, Rightly Dividing the Word, MBI Publishing, 2009

Missler, C. & Eastman, M., Alien Encounters, Koinonia House, 1997.

Pember, G.H., Earth's Earliest Ages, Hodder and Stoughton, 1876 (Reprinted by Kregel Publications, Grand Rapids MI, 1975).

Quale, Stephen, Aliens & Fallen Angels, End Time Thunder Publishers, MT, 2003

Randles, Jenny & Hough, Peter, The Complete Book of UFOs, Sterling Publishing Co., New York 1996.

Spencer, Peter, The DaVinci Cult, BookSurge, 2006

Taylor, Joe. Giants Against Evolution, Mt Blanco Publishing, 2012

Thomas, I.D.E., The Omega Conspiracy, Growth Publishing, Herndon VA, 1986.

Vallee, Jacques, Passport to Magonia, Contemporary Book, Chicago IL, 1993.

Vallee, Jacques, Dimensions, A Casebook of Alien Contact, Ballantine Books, NY, 1988.

Von Daniken, Erich. Twilight of the Gods, New Page Books, 2010

Weldon, J. & Levitt, Z. UFO's: What On Earth Is Happening? Harvest House, 1975

Wilson, Clifford, UFO's and the Mission Impossible, Signet Books - The New American Library of Canada, 1974

Wilson, Clifford, Crash Go The Chariots, Lancer Books, NY, 1972

Wilson, Clifford, The Chariots Still Crash, Signet Books, 1975

Made in the USA
Lexington, KY
22 December 2012